# The Ultimate German Cookbook

## 111 Dishes From Germany To Cook Right Now

### Slavka Bodic

Imprint: Independently published

Please sign up for free Balkan and Mediterranean recipes:
www.balkanfood.org

# Introduction

**D**o you want to enjoy and celebrate the authentic German flavors by cooking some delicious and savory meals at home? Then you have found a perfect read for you! This cookbook will to introduce you to some of the most popular German recipes and meals that you'll definitely love, especially if you're an exotic food lover. Whether you've been to Germany or not, you can recreate its traditional cuisine at home with the help of this comprehensive cookbook. Germany is popular for its unique culture, languages, and food and this book is one good way to come close to the flavorsome cuisine of this European country.

*The Ultimate German Cookbook* will introduce German cuisine and its culinary culture in a way that you may have never experienced before. It brings you a variety of German recipes in one place. The cookbook is great for all those who always wanted to cook German food on their own, without the help of a native German. With this German cuisine cookbook, you can create a complete German menu of your own, or you can try all the special German recipes on different occasions as well. In this cookbook, you'll discover popular German meals and ones that you might not have heard of. From a variety of cakes to the luscious range of pancakes, warming soups, German desserts, drinks, and German salads, etc., you can find them all. What's more, all these recipes are created in such a simple way that those who aren't familiar with the German culture, food, and language can still try and cook them at home without facing much difficulty.

German culinary culture and cuisine are indeed full of wonders. There's great use of sauerkraut, cabbage, beets, and cherries. And, if you want to add all those nutri-dense ingredients to your routine diet, then give this book a thorough read, and you'll uncover all your answers right away.

What you can gain from this cookbook:

- An Overview about German Cuisine
- Insights About Germany
- German Breakfast Recipes
- Appetizers
- Salads and Soups
- Main Dishes
- German desserts and drinks

Let's try all these German recipes and recreate a complete menu to celebrate the amazing German flavors and unforgettable aromas!

# Table of Contents

# Why German Cuisine?

What does German cuisine remind you of? Does it trigger delicious peach kuchen and, or does it conjure the Jaeger Schnitzel? Well, the cuisine has tons of other exciting and delicious meals to offer you. It offers a mix of regional and cultural influence, which makes German cuisine not only special but also quite unique. German food attracts many because of the amazing combination of vegetables, meats, and fruits.

When it comes to German meals, they're made using basic spices, more fermented food and a lot of fruits and vegetables. Most meals are loaded with a number of ingredients. The cuisine focuses on the use of all type of meat, poultry, seafood, vegetables and other agricultural produce. Some fruits and veggies are widely grown in Germany, like potatoes, and that's the reason that potatoes are most commonly used in most German meals. Similarly, cabbage sauerkraut berries, and apples are some popular ingredients in this region. Other commonly used ingredients of German cuisine are:

- Beets
- Pork shanks
- Sauerkraut
- Apples
- Potatoes
- Cherries
- Chicken
- Pork chops

German cuisine is an ancient cuisine that has several cooking techniques that are developed over hundreds of years. It originated with all the native German ingredients, along with those which were brought to this land by the people from nearby Europeans regions. Some of the most popular dishes include:

- Jaeger Schnitzel
- German Sautéed Spaetzle Dumplings
- German Hamburgers (Frikadellen)
- German Pork Chops and Sauerkraut
- German Beef Rouladen
- Oktoberfest Chicken and Red Cabbage
- Sauerbraten
- Wienerschnitzel

Beside these snacks and entrees, you'll savor some amazing German dessert here, like the German Apfelkuchen, German Bee Sting Cake (Bienenstich Kuchen), German Raspberry Dessert, Spaghetti Ice Cream, Christmas Stollen With Almonds, and German Rum Balls (Rumkugeln). If you want to try the German vacation drink or the traditional German glühwein, then it's about time that you make them by yourself.

# Germany

Germany has always been the biggest attraction in Europe, and it remained at the center of the region's history. It's one of the fastest moving economies of Europe and holds a special position on the stage of world politics. This is at least how we all know Germany. What most of us aren't familiar with is the diversity of its cuisine, culture, and amazing people. The region is packed with amazing landscapes and beautiful heritage sites to visit. German universities and education institutes attract millions of students from around the world.

The Federal Republic of Germany that we know as Germany is a country located at the crossroads of Western and Central Europe. It's present between the North and Baltic seas in the north and the Alps of the south. The country covers an area of 357,022 square kilometers with a population of more than 83 million in its 16 states. It shares its borders with Poland and the Czech Republic to the east, Denmark to the north, Austria and Switzerland to the south, and Luxembourg, France, Belgium, and the Netherlands to the west. In fact, it's further the second-most populous country in Europe after Russia and one key member of the European Union. Its largest city and is Berlin, whereas Frankfurt is its financial center. The largest urban hub of the country is the Ruhour.

People who have never been to Germany and never explored many of its places and cities cannot fathom the beauty of its amazing landscapes. Most people get the idea of this land from the movies they watch, but Germany is much more than what you see on the screens. It has some amazing cities and diversely populated urban centers with ancient architecture that are reminiscent of the great Germanic Empire. Some of the best attractions in the country include:

- The Ultimate Fairytale Castle (Neuschwanstein)
- Berlin's Brandenburg Gate

- Cologne Cathedral (Kölner Dom)
- Miniature Wunderland and the Historic Port of Hamburg
- The Rhine Valley
- Berlin's Museum Island
- Bamberg and the Bürgerstadt
- Zugspitze Massif
- The Island of Rugen
- King's Lake (Königssee)

My last visit to Germany delivered several amazing sights and an unforgettable experience of getting to know the German food, the people, and the culture. The whole atmosphere etches your mind and soul into it, and you feel like getting lost in the streets of Berlin and the Black Forest. If you too haven't been to Germany yet, then try its authentic meals and recipes from the cookbook and spread the traditional German aromas all around you.

# Breakfasts

# German Soft Pretzels (Laugenbrezel)

**Preparation time:** 10 minutes
**Cook time:** 20 minutes
**Nutrition facts (per serving):** 232 cal (14g fat, 10g protein, 1.3g fiber)

Enjoy these on your German breakfast menu. These pretzels are super soft on the inside and crispy and golden on the side. They're best served with cream cheese dip.

## Ingredients (6 servings)

2 cups warm water
2 (¼ oz.) packages yeast
2 tablespoon Barley Malt Syrup
6 ½ cups bread flour
2 tablespoon coarse salt
½ cup cold butter, diced
8 cups water
½ cup baking soda
¼ cup dark brown sugar
½ cup pale ale beer
Pretzel salt for sprinkling

## Preparation

Mix warm water with malt syrup and yeast in a mixing bowl and then leave for 10 minutes. Stir in flour, salt, and butter and then mix well in a stand mixer for 6 minutes. Cover the prepared dough bowl and leave it for 2 hours.

At 450 degrees F, preheat your oven. Roll the prepared dough into a large 14x12 inch rectangle and cut it into 12 inches long strips. Roll the dough piece into a 33-inch-long rope and fold into a pretzel shape. Make more pretzels and place them on the baking sheets, greased with cooking spray. Add 8 cups of water, beer, brown sugar, and baking soda to a saucepan, then boil the mixture. Add pretzels to the boiling water for 30 seconds and then transfer to the baking sheets using a slotted spoon. Drizzle salt on top and bake for 5 minutes in the oven. Flip the pretzels and bake for 5 minutes more. Serve.

# German Apple Pancakes

**Preparation time:** 10 minutes
**Cook time:** 20 minutes
**Nutrition facts (per serving):** 216 cal (14g fat, 4g protein, 1g fiber)

The famous German apple pancakes are here to make your breakfast special. You can always serve these pancakes with maple syrup and fresh berries.

## Ingredients (6 servings)

3 tablespoon butter
1 apple, cored and sliced
½ teaspoon cinnamon
5 tablespoon sugar
1 teaspoon lemon zest
3 eggs
⅔ cup milk
⅔ cup flour
⅛ teaspoon salt

## Preparation

At 425 degrees F, preheat your oven. Add the butter and melt in a 10-inch pan over medium heat. Mix the apple slices with cinnamon and 2 tablespoon of sugar in the pan. Next, place in the oven until golden brown. Blend the eggs with lemon zest and 3 tablespoon of sugar in a blender for 1 minute. Stir in the flour, salt, and milk. Then mix until lump-free. Pour this mixture over the apples and bake for 20 minutes in the oven. Garnish and serve.

# German Sandwich with Ham

**Preparation time:** 15 minutes
**Cook time:** 12 minutes
**Nutrition facts (per serving):** 722 cal (57g fat, 36g protein, 4g fiber)

The famous German sandwich with ham is a must on the German menu. Try cooking it at home with these healthy ingredients and enjoy.

## Ingredients (2 servings)
2 tablespoon butter
1 brown rye bread slice
2 oz. ham, sliced
2 oz. Gruyere cheese, sliced
1 egg
1 teaspoon fresh parsley, chopped
Salt and black pepper to taste

## Preparation
Spread 1 tablespoon butter over the bread slice and place it on the serving plate. Sauté the ham in a skillet for 4 minutes. Add Gruyere cheese on top, cook for 2 minutes, and then remove from the heat. Add the remaining butter to a skillet and pour in the egg. Cook for 3 minutes per side. Add ham and cheese on top of the bread slice and top it with the egg. Garnish with parsley, black pepper, and salt. Serve warm.

# German Potato Omelette

**Preparation time:** 15 minutes
**Cook time:** 20 minutes
**Nutrition facts (per serving):** 400 cal (22g fat, 17g protein, 10g fiber)

You can give this potato-filled omelette a try because it has a good and delicious combination of fried eggs and sautéed potatoes as stuffing.

## Ingredients (8 servings)

2 large potatoes, sliced
¼ cup butter
½ cup green onions, sliced
8 large eggs
¼ cup milk
Salt and black pepper to taste

## Preparation

Sauté the potatoes with 2 tablespoon butter in a suitable skillet for 15 minutes. Add the onion, mix, and place the skillet aside. Beat the eggs with milk in a suitable bowl. Set a pan with remaining butter over medium-high heat. Pour in the eggs and cook until set. Add the potatoes on top of one side of the omelette and then fold in half. Slice and serve.

# Dakota Kuchen

**Preparation time:** 5 minutes
**Cook time:** 20 minutes
**Nutrition facts (per serving):** 376 cal (14g fat, 22g protein, 18g fiber)

This German Dakota Kuchen recipe will make your day with its delightful taste. Serve warm with your favorite bread.

## Ingredients (8 servings)
### Dough
2 cups warm milk
½ cup sugar
1 (¼ oz.) package yeast
6 cups flour
½ cup oil
1 teaspoon salt
2 eggs

### Filling
1-quart heavy cream
6 eggs
1 cup of sugar
1 dash salt
Cinnamon sugar mixture

## Preparation
Mix warm milk with sugar and yeast in a bowl. Leave it for 5 minutes and then add flour, oil, salt, and eggs. Mix well until it makes a smooth dough. Cover and leave this dough for 2 hours. Meanwhile, mix all the filling ingredients in a saucepan, cook until it thickens, and then allow it to cool. Divide the prepared dough into small pie pans and spread it evenly. Divide the filling into the crust

and top with cinnamon and sugar. Bake the pies for 20 minutes in the oven at 350 degrees F. Allow them to cool and serve.

# Farmer's Breakfast

**Preparation time:** 15 minutes
**Cook time:** 22 minutes
**Nutrition facts (per serving):** 381 cal (6g fat, 13g protein, 1g fiber)

If you're bored with the usual morning bread, then this German potato breakfast is one unique option to go for. Enjoy it with crispy bacon and eggs.

**Ingredients (2 servings)**
2 medium potato, sliced
1 tablespoon olive oil
1 small onion, chopped
2 large eggs
¼ cup rosemary, fresh, chopped
¼ cup basil, fresh, chopped
Salt and black pepper to taste

**Preparation**
Sauté the potatoes with olive oil in a cooking pan for 15 minutes. Toss in onion, then sautés for 5 minutes. Beat the eggs and pour over the potatoes. Drizzle cheeses, black pepper, salt, and herbs on top. Cook for 2 minutes and then add a splash of vinegar on top. Slice and serve.

# Hopple Popple German Breakfast Casserole

**Preparation time:** 5 minutes
**Cook time:** 17 minutes
**Nutrition facts (per serving):** 206 cal (15g fat, 21g protein, 1g fiber)

Try the German hopple Popple casserole and cook it quickly for your breakfast. Serve this hash brown casserole with all your favorite bread.

## Ingredients (4 servings)
4 cups frozen hash brown potatoes
⅓ cup onion, chopped
4 tablespoon butter
6 eggs
½ cup milk
2 tablespoons mixed Italian herbs
½ teaspoon salt
½ teaspoon pepper
25 pepperoni slices
1 cup sharp cheddar cheese, shredded
1 cup mozzarella cheese, shredded

## Preparation
Sauté the potatoes, butter, and onion in a suitable skillet until brown. Beat the eggs with seasonings and milk in a bowl, and then pour over the potatoes. Spread the pepperoni on top, cover and cook for 15 minutes on medium-low heat. Drizzle cheeses on top, cover and cook for 2 minutes. Slice and serve.

# Potato Pancakes (German Kartoffelpuffer)

**Preparation time:** 15 minutes
**Cook time:** 20 minutes
**Nutrition facts (per serving):** 119 cal (4g fat, 5g protein, 3g fiber)

Here come the classic potato pancakes, which are mostly served at the breakfast or snack table. It has a blend of starchy potatoes and onion.

### Ingredients (4 servings)
2 ½ lbs. starchy potatoes, peeled and grated
1 small yellow onion, grated
2 large eggs
¼ cup all-purpose flour
1 teaspoon sea salt
Cooking oil for frying

### Preparation
Squeeze the liquid from the potato grates and transfer to a bowl. Stir in the flour, salt, eggs and grated onion. Mix well and take ½ cup mixture to make each flat pancake. Set a skillet with cooking oil over medium heat and sear the pancakes for 5 minutes per side. Serve warm.

# Apple Cinnamon Kaiserschmarrns

**Preparation time:** 10 minutes
**Cook time:** 15 minutes
**Nutrition facts (per serving):** 368 cal (11g fat, 12g protein, 1g fiber)

Do you want to enjoy some pancake rolls with your favorite toppings on top? These apple cinnamon rolls are quick to make and easy to serve.

## Ingredients (6 servings)
6 eggs
1 cup milk
1 ½ cups four
3/8 cups sugar
Butter for frying
Fruit Jam for filling
Powdered sugar for sprinkling

## Preparation
Mix the eggs with flour, sugar, and milk in a large bowl until smooth. Set a 12-inch skillet with butter over medium heat. Pour in ¾ cup batter, spread it and cook for 2 minutes per side. Dust with sugar and serve with jam. Enjoy.

# German Semolina Pudding (Griessbrei)

**Preparation time:** 10 minutes
**Cook time:** 10 minutes
**Nutrition facts (per serving):** 244 cal (10g fat, 8g protein, 2.5g fiber)

This semolina pudding is a classic German meal, great for breakfast, and for side meals. You can try this pudding with cinnamon and fruits on top.

**Ingredients (2 servings)**
1 ½ cups milk
1 teaspoon vanilla extract
2 tablespoon sugar
1 oz. semolina

**Preparation**
Mix milk with vanilla and sugar in a saucepan. Set this pan over medium-high heat and let it boil. Reduce the heat and then stir in the semolina. Cook for 5 minutes with occasional stirring until it thickens. Remove the pan from the heat and allow it to cool. Serve.

# German Eggs in Mustard Sauce

**Preparation time:** 15 minutes
**Cook time:** 10 minutes
**Nutrition facts (per serving):** 320 cal (25g fat, 15g protein, 5.4g fiber)

It's about time to try some German eggs in mustard sauce on the breakfast menu and make it taste more diverse in flavors. Serve warm with your favorite herbs on top.

## Ingredients (8 servings)
8 large eggs, hard-boiled and peeled
2 tablespoon butter
1 oz. all-purpose flour
1 cup vegetable broth
⅓ cup double cream
2 tablespoon Dijon mustard
1 tablespoon fresh lemon juice
2 pinches sugar
4 tablespoon dill, fresh, chopped

## Preparation
Cut all the half-boiled eggs in half. Sauté the flour with butter in a saucepan for 2 minutes. Stir in the vegetable broth, cream, Dijon mustard, lemon juice and sugar. Cook with occasional stirring until the sauce thickens. Add the eggs to the mustard sauce and garnish with herbs. Serve warm.

# German Waffles

**Preparation time:** 15 minutes
**Cook time:** 14 minutes
**Nutrition facts (per serving):** 306 cal (15g fat, 7g protein, 2g fiber)

The German breakfast waffles is a delicious morning meal you can try every day; it's best to serve with maple syrup or butter on top. You can try other toppings as well.

## Ingredients (4 servings)
3 eggs
1 pinch salt
½ cup unsalted butter
½ cup sugar
1 tablespoon vanilla sugar
2 cups flour
¼ teaspoon baking powder
1 cup milk
½ cup of mineral water
Cherry sauce
Whipped cream

## Preparation
Beat the egg whites with salt in a bowl until fluffy. Mix the butter with sugar and vanilla in a bowl until creamy. Beat in the egg yolks and sugar and then mix until smooth. Stir in the baking powder and flour. Add the butter mixture and milk and then mix until lump-free. Fold in the egg whites and mix gently. Preheat your waffle iron as per the instructions and add a ladle of batter into the iron. Cook for 7 minutes, then transfer to a plate. Cook more waffles in the same way. Serve with your desired toppings. Enjoy.

# North German Franz Buns

**Preparation time:** 15 minutes
**Cook time:** 15 minutes
**Nutrition facts (per serving):** 213 cal (20g fat, 12g protein, 7g fiber)

The German breakfast Franz buns are prepared with basic baking ingredients, yet they taste so delicious. Serve these buns with crispy bacon or eggs.

## Ingredients (6 servings)
4 cups flour
1 fresh cube yeast
1 cup lukewarm milk
1 ⅓ cups packed brown sugar
3 egg yolks
1 pinch of salt
⅓ cup butter softened
¾ cup 2 tablespoon butter chilled
2 teaspoon cinnamon

## Preparation
Mix yeast and milk in a bowl and leave it for 15 minutes. Stir in 2 egg yolks, ⅓ cup sugar, salt, and ⅓ cup soft butter, and then mix well. Stir in the flour and mix until smooth. Knead this dough for 5 minutes. Cover this dough with a plastic sheet and leave it for 45 minutes. Knead the prepared dough again, transfer it to a working surface, and spread it into a 12x27 inches rectangle. Mix the cinnamon with the remaining sugar in a bowl and cut in butter. Spread the cinnamon mixture over the prepared dough. Roll the rectangle and cut this roll into 2-inch-thick slices. Place the buns in a baking tray lined with parchment paper. Cover and leave these rolls for 15 minutes. At 360 degrees F, preheat your oven. Beat the remaining egg yolk with a tablespoon of milk and brush the mixture over the rolls. Bake the rolls for 15 minutes in the oven. Serve.

# German Potato Breakfast Casserole

**Preparation time:** 10 minutes
**Cook time:** 45 minutes
**Nutrition facts (per serving):** 321 cal (10g fat, 12g protein, 2g fiber)

It's as if the German menu is incomplete without this potato breakfast casserole. It's Germany's special inspired morning meal to serve.

**Ingredients (8 servings)**
2 cans German Potato Salad
8 large eggs
½ cup cream
1 cup cheddar cheese, shredded
¼ teaspoon black pepper
¼ teaspoon sea salt
½ bell pepper, sliced
3 scallions, diced

**Preparation**
At 350 degrees F, preheat your oven. Drain the potato salad and remove excess liquid. Grease a 10-inch skillet with cooking spray. Spread the potato salad in the skillet. Mix the eggs with cream, cheddar, black pepper, salt, bell pepper, and scallions in a bowl. Pour the mixture on top of the potato salad. Bake for 35 minutes in the oven, then cover the casserole with a foil sheet. Bake for 10 minutes Serve warm.

# German Breakfast Pancakes

**Preparation time:** 15 minutes
**Cook time:** 20 minutes
**Nutrition facts (per serving):** 242 cal (14g fat, 12g protein, 1g fiber)

This blueberry pancake is another good choice for the morning table that's famous in Germany. It's prepared using the basic baking ingredients along with fresh berry garnishing.

## Ingredients (6 servings)

⅔ cup all-purpose flour
⅔ cup whole milk
3 large eggs
3 tablespoon granulated sugar
1 pinch of salt
4 tablespoon unsalted butter
¾ cup raspberries
¾ cup blackberries
Toasted sliced almonds for serving
Confectioners' sugar, for dusting

## Preparation

At 400 degrees F, preheat your oven. Set a 10-inch cast-iron skillet in the oven to preheat. Mix the flour with salt, sugar, eggs, and milk in a bowl until smooth. Add the butter to the heated pan and pour in the batter. Bake this batter for 20 minutes. Garnish with berries, almonds, and sugar. Slice and serve.

# German Morning Crepes

**Preparation time:** 10 minutes
**Cook time:** 10 minutes
**Nutrition facts (per serving):** 243 cal (11g fat, 15g protein, 1g fiber)

Best to serve at breakfast, these German crepes can be served as a morning meal with eggs and crispy bacon. It's rich and loaded with healthy fats.

## Ingredients (4 servings)
### Batter
5 tablespoon flour
4 tablespoon granulated sugar
2 eggs
1 teaspoon vanilla extract
¼ teaspoon salt
1 cup milk

### Filling
1 can fruit, drained
8 oz. cream cheese
3 tablespoon powdered sugar
2 tablespoon cream
1 teaspoon lemon peel, grated

## Preparation
Mix the flour with sugar, eggs, vanilla extract, salt, and milk in a bowl until lump-free. Leave this batter for 30 minutes. Meanwhile, prepare the filling and beat cream cheese with lemon peel, cream and sugar in a bowl. Stir in fruit and keep this filling aside. Grease a suitable pan with butter or oil and set it over medium heat. Pour a ladle of this batter into the pan, spread it around and cook for 1-2 minutes per side. Make more crepes in the same way and transfer to a

plate. Add a tablespoon of the filling at the center of each crepe, and then roll. Serve with cream on top. Enjoy.

# Appetizers and Snacks

# German Currywurst

**Preparation time:** 15 minutes
**Cook time:** 20 minutes
**Nutrition facts (per serving):** 451 cal (32g fat, 18g protein, 1g fiber)

The German currywurst is one of the most delicious street foods that you can try at home. It's known for its saucy taste and the energizing combination of ingredients.

## Ingredients (6 servings)

3 (15 oz.) cans tomato sauce
1-lb. kielbasa
2 tablespoon chili sauce
½ teaspoon onion salt
1 tablespoon white sugar
1 teaspoon black pepper
1 pinch paprika
Curry powder to taste

## Preparation

Preheat the oven on Broil mode. Add the tomato sauce, chili sauce, black pepper, sugar, salt, and onion to a saucepan. Cook the mixture on a simmer for 5 minutes until reduced to half. Place the sausage in a baking sheet and broil for 4 minutes per side. Slice the broiled sausages and pour the tomato sauce on top. Drizzle with curry powder and paprika. Serve warm.

# German Potato Pasta (Badische Schupfnudeln)

**Preparation time:** 10 minutes
**Cook time:** 40 minutes
**Nutrition facts (per serving):** 357 cal (24g fat, 12g protein, 0g fiber)

Have you ever tried German potato pasta? Well, here's a recipe to make some delicious potato pasta. Enjoy with your favorite sauce.

### Ingredients (4 servings)
1-lb. potatoes
2 tablespoon flour
2 egg yolks
Dash grated nutmeg
½ teaspoon salt
2 tablespoon butter

### Preparation
Boil the potatoes in a pot filled with boiling water and cook for 30 minutes. Peel the potatoes once cooked and pass them through a ricer. Mix the flour with salt, nutmeg, and egg yolks in a bowl until smooth. Add more flour if needed to get smooth dough. Leave the prepared dough to rest for 15 minutes. Place this dough on a floured surface and shape it into a log. Cut this log into 20 pieces. Shape each piece into a cylinder and tapper both ends of the small cylinders. Sauté this pasta in a cooking pan greased with butter until golden brown. Serve warm.

# Bavarian Beer Cheese

**Preparation time:** 10 minutes
**Nutrition facts (per serving):** 282 cal (16g fat, 11g protein, 2g fiber)

German beer cheese is a cheesy dip which makes as excellent serving with tortilla chips and all other snacks.

## Ingredients (6 servings)
8 oz. Camembert cheese
8 oz. spreadable cheese
⅓ cup butter
2 ½ teaspoon sweet paprika
2 teaspoon caraway seed, ground
Salt and black pepper to taste
¼ cup Dunkel lager
⅓ cup onion, chopped
1 small bunch chives, chopped

## Preparation
Mix the camembert with salt, black pepper, beer, caraway seeds, paprika, butter, and spreadable cheese in a bowl with a fork. Cover the mixture with a plastic sheet and refrigerate for 3 hours. Uncover and add chives and onion. Mix well and garnish with chives. Serve.

# German Meatballs (Frikadellen)

**Preparation time:** 15 minutes
**Cook time:** 10 minutes
**Nutrition facts (per serving):** 299 cal (8g fat, 28g protein, 1g fiber)

These loaded meatballs are here to complete your German menu. These meatballs are served as a side meal on all special occasions and celebrations.

Ingredients (8 servings)
1 bread roll
1 onion, diced
1 tablespoon cooking oil
3 tablespoon parsley, chopped
10 oz. ground pork
10 oz. ground beef
1 tablespoon German mustard
1 egg
1 teaspoon salt
½ teaspoon black pepper
½ tablespoon paprika
2 teaspoon dried marjoram
1 cup cooking oil for frying

## Preparation

Soak the bread roll in water in a bowl for 20 minutes, then crumble. Sauté the onion with 1 tablespoon cooking oil in a cooking pan over medium heat until soft, then remove from the heat. Stir in parsley and mix well. Transfer this mixture to the crumbled roll. Stir in marjoram, paprika, black pepper, salt, mustard, ground meat, egg, and the rest of the ingredients before mixing well. Make equal-sized patties out of this mixture. Sear the patties in a skillet with cooking oil for 5 minutes per side. Serve.

# Smoked Trout Dip

**Preparation time:** 10 minutes
**Nutrition facts (per serving):** 241 cal (24g fat, 22g protein, 1.1g fiber)

Here comes a German smoked trout dip that's beloved by all. The cream cheese base is mixed with trout fillets and capers along with spices and herbs.

## Ingredients (12 servings)
8 oz. smoked trout fillets
8 oz. cream cheese
1 tablespoon capers
1 teaspoon dried dill weed
1 teaspoon paprika
1 lemon, zest and juice
2 tablespoon fresh chives, chopped
Salt and black pepper, to taste

## Preparation
Blend cream cheese, chives, and the rest of the ingredients in a bowl. Serve.

# Pickled Eggs

**Preparation time:** 15 minutes
**Cook time:** 45 minutes
**Nutrition facts (per serving):** 296 cal (6g fat, 23g protein, 2g fiber)

Pickled eggs are a popular German snack and side meal that are enjoyed all over the country. They blend a delightful mix of eggs soaked in a homemade brine solution.

**Ingredients (10 servings)**
10 eggs, hardboiled and peeled

*Beet Pickled Eggs*
1 cup apple cider vinegar
3 small beets
¼ cup beet juice
¾ cups water
1 tablespoon sugar
2 bay leaves
1 teaspoon mustard seeds
Cloves, black peppercorns to taste

**Preparation**
Boil the beets in a cooking pot filled with water for 40 minutes then remove the beets from the liquid. Slice the beet and transfer to a mason jar. Add the peeled eggs to the beets. Add water, salt, sugar, vinegar, bay leaf, beef juice, peppercorns, cloves, and mustard seeds to the beets' liquid. Cook for 5 minutes then strain this liquid. Pour this liquid in to the jar then cover the lid. Refrigerate overnight and serve.

# German Cottage Fries (Bratkartoffeln)

**Preparation time:** 5 minutes
**Cook time:** 35 minutes
**Nutrition facts (per serving):** 231 cal (11g fat, 10g protein, 0.3g fiber)

German cottage fries make a great serving if you're seeking f a quick snack to make. Serve these fries with delicious cream cheese dip.

### Ingredients (4 servings)
2 lbs. firm potatoes, sliced
1 small onion, sliced
6 thick-cut bacon, strips
2 tablespoon cooking oil
Salt and black pepper, to taste
1 tablespoon fresh herb, chopped

### Preparation
Boil the potatoes in a saucepan filled with water until soft and then drain. Sauté the bacon in a pan until crispy and then transfer to a plate. Sauté the onion in the same pan until soft. Stir in the cooking oil, potatoes, black pepper, salt, and herbs, then sauté for 5 minutes. Crumble the bacon on top of the potatoes and serve.

# White Asparagus With Hollandaise Sauce

**Preparation time:** 15 minutes
**Cook time:** 30 minutes
**Nutrition facts (per serving):** 354 cal (35g fat, 5g protein, 1.4g fiber)

If you haven't tried the white asparagus with hollandaise sauce before, then here comes a simple and easy to cook recipe that you can easily prepare and cook at home in no time with minimum efforts.

**Ingredients (6 servings)**
*White Asparagus*
1 lb. white asparagus
1 tablespoon butter
1 teaspoon salt
1 teaspoon sugar
1 tablespoon lemon juice

*Hollandaise Sauce*
10 tablespoon butter
3 egg yolks
1 tablespoon white wine
1 tablespoon lemon juice
½ teaspoon salt
½ teaspoon hot sauce

**Preparation**
Add the asparagus, butter, sugar, salt, and lemon juice to a cooking pot filled with water. Cook for 20 minutes and then drain. Place the asparagus spears on the serving plate. For the sauce, melt butter in a saucepan. Beat the egg yolks, hot sauce, white wine, salt, and lemon juice in a blender. Continue beating this sauce and melted butter until completely incorporated. Pour this sauce over the asparagus. Serve.

# German Onion Pie (Zwiebelkuchen)

**Preparation time:** 15 minutes
**Cook time:** 51 minutes
**Nutrition facts (per serving):** 275 cal (9g fat, 21g protein, 2g fiber)

This German onion pie, loaded with bacon and cream filling, is another German-inspired delight that you should definitely try on this Cuisine. Serve with chili garlic sauce.

**Ingredients (6 servings)**
*Dough for Crust*
1 packet dry active yeast
⅔ cup milk, lukewarm
1 teaspoon sugar
2 cups flour
1 teaspoon salt
¼ cup butter

*Filling*
4 oz. bacon, diced
1 lb. onions, chopped
2 tablespoon butter
1 tablespoon flour
2 eggs
½ cup heavy cream
2 teaspoon salt
1 pinch of nutmeg
Caraway seed, to taste

**Preparation**
Mix the yeast with sugar and milk in a bowl and then leave it for 5 minutes. Stir in the flour and salt before mixing well until smooth. Knead this dough on the

working surface, place it in a glass bowl, and then cover it with a plastic sheet. Leave the prepared dough for 2 hours. Knead the prepared dough again and roll the prepared dough into a 9-inch round. Sauté bacon in a cooking pan until crispy. Transfer to a plate and add butter and onions to the same pan. Sauté until soft, then add 1 tablespoon flour, and sauté for 1 minute. At 400 degrees F, preheat your oven. Beat the eggs with salt, cream, and nutmeg in a bowl. Stir in the bacon and onion mixture. Place the prepared dough round in a greased 10-inch pie plate. Add the onion filling to the crust and top it with caraway seeds and butter. Bake for 45 minutes in the oven. Slice and serve.

# Sausage Bites Appetizer

**Preparation time:** 15 minutes
**Cook time:** 17 minutes
**Nutrition facts (per serving):** 245 cal (10g fat, 13g protein, 2g fiber)

These simple, quick and easy sausage bites appetizer have no parallel. If you have some crescent dough sheet ready at home, then you can prepare it in no time.

## Ingredients (6 servings)
1 tube crescent dough sheet
4 links of pre-cooked sausage
1 egg
1 tablespoon beer
½ tablespoon caraway seeds

## Preparation
At 375 degrees F, preheat your oven. Unroll the crescent dough into a sheet over the cutting board. Place the sausages at the center of the prepared dough sheet and wrap the sheet over the sausages. Cut the roll into bites. Place the bites in a baking sheet lined with parchment paper. Beat the egg and beer in a bowl and then brush on top of the bites. Drizzle the caraway seeds on top. Bake the bites for 17 minutes in the oven until golden brown. Serve.

# Sauerkraut Strudel

**Preparation time:** 10 minutes
**Cook time:** 45 minutes
**Nutrition facts (per serving):** 274 cal (3g fat, 11g protein, 3g fiber)

Have you tried the famous sauerkraut strudel? If you haven't, now is the time to cook this delicious strudel at home using simple and healthy ingredients.

### Ingredients (6 servings)
1 package puff pastry
4 tablespoon butter, melted
6 bacon slices, diced
1 onion, diced
1 egg
2 tablespoon bread crumbs
2 cups drained sauerkraut
Caraway seeds, to taste
Cumin, to taste

### Preparation
At 350 degrees F, preheat your oven. Sauté the bacon in a pan until crispy and then transfer to a plate. Add the onion to the same pan and sauté until soft, and then allow it to cool. Stir in the sauerkraut, seasonings, bread crumbs, egg, onion, and bacon. Mix well and keep the filling aside. Unroll the pastry sheets on the working surface. Top both sheets with the filling and roll them. Tuck the rolls' ends and places them in a baking sheet, greased with butter. Bake the rolls for 35 minutes in the oven until golden brown. Slice and serve.

# Salads

# Limburger Cheese Salad

**Preparation time:** 10 minutes
**Nutrition facts (per serving):** 261 cal (3g fat, 15g protein, 1g fiber)

The German Limburger cheese salad is a rich delight that you can easily prepare at home. The salad is fairly easy to make and doesn't require any cooking.

## Ingredients (4 servings)
12 oz. Limburger cheese, sliced
2 tablespoon vegetable oil
2 tablespoon sherry vinegar
1 small onion, sliced in rings
2 tablespoon sweet paprika
Salt and black pepper, to taste
1 teaspoon caraway seeds

## Preparation
Mix the oil with vinegar, onion, paprika, salt, and black pepper in a small bowl. Place the cheese slices on the serving platter. Pour the dressing on top. Drizzle with caraway seeds and serve.

# German Sausage Salad

**Preparation time:** 10 minutes
**Nutrition facts (per serving):** 302 cal (11g fat, 12g protein, 5g fiber)

The German sausage salad is enjoyed with all sorts of entrees, and it tastes great with sour cream on top. Have it in your dinner table for a tempting serving.

## Ingredients (6 servings)

½ lb. bologna, sliced
½ small red onion, sliced
5 small pickles, sliced
½ small apple, sliced
1 tablespoon parsley

### Dressing

3 tablespoon sunflower oil
1 tablespoon white wine vinegar
1 tablespoon sugar
Salt and black pepper, to taste

## Preparation

Toss all the dressing ingredients in a salad bowl. Stir in the bologna, red onion, pickles, apple, and parsley. Mix well and serve.

# German Red Cabbage (Rot kohl)

**Preparation time:** 10 minutes
**Cook time:** 1 hour 15 minutes
**Nutrition facts (per serving):** 178 cal (10g fat, 4g protein, 2g fiber)

If you can't think of anything delicious and savory to serve, then try this red cabbage because it has great taste and texture for a German treat.

## Ingredients (4 servings)
2 tablespoon butter
1 yellow onion, chopped
1 large apple, peeled and chopped
1 head red cabbage, sliced
3 tablespoon red wine vinegar
1 cup apple cider
1 tablespoon granulated sugar
1 bay leaf
2 whole cloves
2 juniper berries
½ teaspoon salt

## Preparation
Sauté the onion and apples with butter in a Dutch oven over medium-high heat and cook for 10 minutes. Stir in the cabbage and sauté for 5 minutes. Stir in the rest of the ingredients, boil the mixture, cover, and reduce its heat to cook for 1 hour on a simmer. Serve warm.

# Radish Salad

**Preparation time:** 5 minutes
**Nutrition facts (per serving):** 149 cal (1g fat, 9g protein, 0.1g fiber)

Radish salad is everyone's favorite go-to side meal. Full of great taste and benefits, it's easy to make and doesn't tons of ingredients.

## Ingredients (2 servings)
1 radish
1 teaspoon chives, chopped

## Preparation
Pass the radish through the spiralizer and cut into thin rounds. Spread the shavings onto the serving platter. Drizzle chives on top and serve.

# German Coleslaw Salad

**Preparation time:** 10 minutes
**Cook time:** 5 minutes
**Nutrition facts (per serving):** 51 cal (4g fat, 1g protein, 1g fiber)

This German coleslaw has a delightful mix of cooked cabbage with bacon and herbs. Serve this mix with all your entrees and a drizzle of pepper on top.

## Ingredients (6 servings)
1 small white cabbage, shredded
⅔ cup vegetable stock
¼ cup apple cider vinegar
1 teaspoon sugar
1 teaspoon caraway seeds
1 ½ tablespoon olive oil
Salt, to taste
White pepper, to taste
4 bacon slices, cooked and crumbled
2 teaspoon parsley, chopped

## Preparation
Boil the vegetable stock with caraway seeds, sugar, and vinegar in a saucepan and then remove from the heat. Stir and mix until dissolved. Add cabbage and leave the mixture for 15 minutes. Drain in the cabbage and toss with the rest of the ingredients in a salad bowl. Serve.

# German Cucumber Salad

**Preparation time:** 15 minutes
**Nutrition facts (per serving):** 144 cal (17g fat, 16g protein, 1g fiber)

The refreshing cucumber salad is here to make your dinner menu a little more delicious and nourishing.

## Ingredients (4 servings)

2 English cucumbers, peeled and sliced
½ cup sour cream
1 tablespoon white vinegar
1 teaspoon sugar
1 tablespoon dill, fresh or frozen
½ teaspoon salt
Black pepper, to taste

## Preparation

Mix sour cream with vinegar, sugar, dill, salt, and black pepper in a salad bowl. Stir in the cucumber slices. Cover and refrigerate overnight. Serve.

# German Potato Salad

**Preparation time:** 15 minutes
**Cook time:** 25 minutes
**Nutrition facts (per serving):** 183 cal (4g fat, 5g protein, 0.1g fiber)

The appetizing and savory potato salad makes a great addition to the side menu, and it looks fabulous when served at the table.

## Ingredients (6 servings)
3 cups potatoes, peeled and diced
4 bacon slices
1 small onion, diced
¼ cup white vinegar
2 tablespoon water
3 tablespoon white sugar
1 teaspoon salt
⅛ teaspoon black pepper
1 tablespoon fresh parsley, chopped

## Preparation
Add the potatoes to a pot filled with water and boil for 10 minutes until the potatoes are soft. Drain and allow the potatoes to cool. Sauté the bacon in a skillet until brown and crispy. Transfer the bacon to a plate and allow it to cool. Add the onion to the same skillet and sauté until brown. Stir in black pepper, salt, sugar, water, and vinegar. Cook this mixture to a boil, add the potatoes and parsley, and then sauté for 1 minute. Crumble the crispy bacon on top. Serve.

# Celery Root Salad

**Preparation time:** 10 minutes
**Cook time:** 5 minutes
**Nutrition facts (per serving):** 223 cal (5g fat, 14g protein, 1g fiber)

Here comes a fiber-rich mix of all native German ingredients, including celery roots, mustard, and onion. Serve this salad with a drizzle of fresh lemon juice on top.

## Ingredients (4 servings)

3 fresh celery roots
½ cup champagne vinegar
1 tablespoon German hot mustard
¼ cup canola oil
1 medium onion, sliced
Salt and white pepper to taste
2 tablespoon fresh chives, chopped

## Preparation

Add celery roots to a cooking pot filled with water. Cover and cook on medium heat until soft. Drain, peel, and cut the celery roots in julienne. Transfer the celery roots to a salad bowl. Mix vinegar, salt, white pepper, onion, ¼ cup water, and mustard in a small bowl. Pour this dressing over the celery and mix gently. Garnish with chives and serve.

# Purple Potato Salad with Pickled Herring

**Preparation time:** 10 minutes
**Cook time:** 27 minutes
**Nutrition facts (per serving):** 253 cal (18g g fat, 29g protein, 3g fiber)

The famous purple potato salad with herring is fabulous as a healthy side meal. Try making it at home with these healthy ingredients and enjoy it.

## Ingredients (6 servings)
### Salad
1-lb. purple potatoes, sliced
4 tablespoon olive oil
2 shallots, minced
1 teaspoon garlic, minced
2 teaspoon hot German mustard
2 tablespoon sugar
2 teaspoon fennel greens, chopped
2 teaspoon chives, chopped
½ cup vinegar
Sea salt, to taste
Black pepper, to taste
8 oz. mesclun greens
1 jar pickled herring

### Herbed Double Crème
8 oz. double crème
1 teaspoon raspberry vinegar
½ teaspoon dill, chopped
½ teaspoon parsley, chopped
½ teaspoon thyme, chopped
1 tablespoon shallots, chopped
1 garlic clove, minced

Sea salt, to taste
Ground white pepper, to taste

### *Chive Oil*
4 oz. chives, chopped
1 cup grapeseed oil

### Preparation
Soak the potato slices in cold water for 15 minutes and then drain. Prepare the double crème by mixing all its ingredients in a bowl. Prepare the chive oil by mixing its ingredients in a bowl. Sauté the shallots and garlic with 1 tablespoon oil in a cooking pot until soft. Stir in the potatoes and sauté for 2 minutes. Add vinegar and ⅛ cup cold water, then reduce the heat. Cook for 10 minutes. Add the sugar, mustard, chives, greens, remaining oil, black pepper, and salt. Mix well and serve with double crème and chives oil on top. Enjoy.

# Summer Salad

**Preparation time:** 10 minutes
**Nutrition facts (per serving):** 243 cal (13g fat, 4g protein, 0.2g fiber)

This colorful summer salad is a German specialty, and it's served on all special occasions. It's prepared using a nice mix of bell peppers, mushrooms, tomatoes, and lettuce.

## Ingredients (4 servings)
4 eggs, boiled and peeled
2 bell peppers, chopped
1 seedless cucumber, chopped
3 ½ oz. button mushrooms, chopped
⅓ lb. cherry tomatoes, cut in half
1 head lettuce, shredded
1 bunch fresh chives, chopped
2 sprigs fresh dill, chopped
6 tablespoon red wine vinegar
6 tablespoon rapeseed oil
Salt and black pepper, to taste

## Preparation
Toss all the summer salad ingredients in a salad bowl and serve.

# Red Cabbage Orange Salad with Cream Cheese Roulade

**Preparation time:** 10 minutes
**Cook time:** 10 minutes
**Nutrition facts (per serving):** 252 cal (11g fat, 17g protein, 5g fiber)

The loaded red cabbage orange salad is one delicious way to complete your German menu; here's a recipe that you can try for a memorable meal.

## Ingredients (6 servings)
*Cream cheese roulade*
1 ¼ cup of all-purpose flour
1 cup milk
2 eggs
1 tablespoon vegetable oil
1 dash salt
¼ teaspoon nutmeg, grated
Butter to bake pancakes
¼ cup cream cheese
¼ cup herb cheese

## *Salad*
1 jar Hengstenberg red cabbage
3 oranges, cut into sections
Salt and black pepper to taste
5 tablespoon sunflower oil
1 chicory to garnish

## Preparation
Mix the four with eggs and milk in a bowl. Stir in the nutmeg, salt, and oil. Mix until it makes a smooth dough. Make four (9 inch) pancakes from this mixture. Mix the sour cream with herb cheese and cream cheese in a bowl. Spread this

mixture on top of the pancakes. Roll all the pancakes, wrap in plastic, and allow them to refrigerate. Toss all the salad ingredients in a salad bowl. Cut the cheese roulade into thin strips and place on top of the salad. Serve.

# Sesame Spaetzle Salad

**Preparation time:** 10 minutes
**Nutrition facts (per serving):** 207 cal (8g fat, 13g protein, 1g fiber)

This sesame spaetzle salad makes a great side for the table, and you can serve it with delicious and healthy entrees as well.

## Ingredients (4 servings)
⅓ cup vinegar
⅓ cup scallions, sliced
¼ cup soy sauce
¼ cup honey
1 tablespoon ginger root, grated
1 tablespoon garlic-chili pepper sauce
1 9-oz. package spaetzle
1 tablespoon toasted sesame oil
1 tablespoon toasted sesame seeds
⅓ cup drained red cabbage
⅓ cup fresh snow peas, sliced
⅓ cup yellow sweet bell pepper, sliced
⅓ cup drained baby corn, sliced
Fresh cilantro, chopped

## Preparation
Toss all the spaetzle salad ingredients in a salad bowl and serve.

# German Potato and Lentil Salad

**Preparation time:** 10 minutes
**Cook time:** 25 minutes
**Nutrition facts (per serving):** 280 cal (5g fat, 12g protein, 2g fiber)

This German potato and lentil salad are made primarily from boiled potatoes, red lentils, and pearl onions, which are then seasoned with vinegar and mustard. The salad tastes great when served with sour cream and croutons.

## Ingredients (4 servings)
1-lb. boiling potatoes peeled
½ cup dry red lentils, rinsed
¼ cup German pickled pearl onions, chopped
1 German dill pickle, chopped
2 tablespoon fresh parsley, minced
¼ tablespoon olive oil
1 tablespoon Bavarian beer vinegar
1 tablespoon German mustard
Salt and black pepper to taste

## Preparation
Add the lentils and potatoes to a large saucepan and pour enough water to cover them. Cook the mixture to a boil and then reduce the heat. Cook for 25 minutes then drain. Dice the cooked potatoes and transfer them to a bowl. Add the onions, parsley, and pickle. Stir in the rest of the ingredients, including the boiled lentils. Serve.

# Soups

# German Potato Soup

**Preparation time:** 10 minutes
**Cook time:** 49 minutes
**Nutrition facts (per serving):** 327 cal (15g fat, 10g protein, 1g fiber)

If you haven't tried the classic German potato soup before, then here comes a simple and easy to cook recipe that you can recreate at home in no time with minimum efforts.

## Ingredients (6 servings)

8 oz. bacon, diced
1 large onion, chopped
1 garlic clove, minced
2 lbs. potatoes, chopped
1 large leek, sliced
3 carrots, diced
1 ½ cups celeriac, diced
2 tomatoes, diced
6 cups quality chicken broth
½ teaspoon dried thyme
½ teaspoon dried rosemary
½ teaspoon dried marjoram
¾ teaspoon sea salt
½ teaspoon black pepper
1 bay leaf
¼ cup fresh parsley, chopped

## Preparation

Sauté the onion with bacon in a pan for 8 minutes. Stir in the garlic and sauté for 1 minute. Stir in rest of the ingredients, except the parsley. Cover and cook on a simmer for 40 minutes. Add black pepper and salt. Finally, garnish with parsley. Serve warm.

# Green Pea Soup with Frankfurters

**Preparation time:** 15 minutes
**Cook time:** 18 minutes
**Nutrition facts (per serving):** 357 cal (10g fat, 13g protein, 2g fiber)

The German pea soup with frankfurter is famous for its unique taste and aroma, and now you can bring those exotic flavors home by using this recipe.

## Ingredients (6 servings)
3 lbs. frozen peas
4 oz. unsalted butter
3 leeks, chopped
4 cups chicken stock, hot
2 cups chicken stock, chilled
1 ¼ cups double cream
14 oz. cooked frankfurter sausages or hot dog, sliced
Croutons fried in butter to serve

## Preparation
Place the peas in a colander and rinse underwater. Sauté the leeks with butter in a cooking pan for 15 minutes until soft. Stir in the peas and the hot chicken stock. Cook the mixture to a boil and cook for 3 minutes. Pour in the cold chicken stock and then blend the soup until smooth. Add cream and mix well. Garnish with frankfurter sausages (or hot dogs) and croutons. Serve.

# German Vegetable Beef Soup

**Preparation time:** 15 minutes
**Cook time:** 35 minutes
**Nutrition facts (per serving):** 167 cal (4 g fat, 11 g protein, 2.8g fiber)

Yes, you can make something as delicious as this vegetable beef soup by using some popular German ingredients like beef, onions, and sauerkraut.

## Ingredients (4 servings)
1 lb. boneless beef, diced
1 cup green pepper, sliced
1 cup corn, fresh or frozen
¾ cup carrots, sliced
½ cup celery, chopped
1 small onion, chopped
½ head cabbage, chopped
6 beef bouillon cubes
8 cups of water
3 10oz. cans tomato juice
¼ cup peas
½ cup green beans
Salt and black pepper, to taste

## Preparation
Sauté the onions and beef in a Dutch oven over medium heat until brown. Mix the bouillon with water and pour over the beef. Stir in the green pepper, cabbage, potatoes, carrots, celery, tomato juice, bay leaf, garlic, black pepper, and salt. Cook for 25 minutes on a simmer. Stir in the peas, beans, and corn, and then discard the bay leaf. Serve warm.

# German Potato Cream Soup (Kartoffelsuppe)

**Preparation time:** 15 minutes
**Cook time:** 25 minutes
**Nutrition facts (per serving):** 381cal (26g fat, 14g protein, 0.6g fiber)

The German potato cream soup has no parallel in taste. It has a mix of potatoes, cream, and butter. Enjoy this soup with a crispy bread.

## Ingredients (4 servings)
2 tablespoon olive oil
2 garlic cloves, sliced
1 small onion, sliced
1 medium carrot, diced
1 stalk celery, diced
1 lb. potatoes, diced
3 cups stock
1 bay leaf
¾ cup double cream
1 tablespoon butter, chilled
1 lemon, grated zest
¼ cup spring onions, cut into thin rings
Salt and pepper, to taste
1 dash cumin powder
1 dash nutmeg powder

## Preparation
Sauté the onion and garlic with olive oil in a cooking pot until soft. Stir in celery and carrot then cook for 5 minutes. Add the bay leaf, stock, and potatoes. Next, cover the lid and cook to a boil. Reduce the heat and cook until the potatoes are soft. Discard the bay leaf and transfer ⅓ of the vegetable mixture to a bowl. Add the butter and double cream to the remaining soup and blend until smooth.

Return the reserved vegetables to the soup. Stir in the lemon zest, black pepper, and salt. Lastly, mix well. Garnish with spring onion and serve warm.

# Chilled Black Cherry Soup

**Preparation time:** 15 minutes
**Cook time:** 15 minutes
**Nutrition facts (per serving):** 248 cal (8g fat, 12g protein, 1g fiber)

A perfect mix of black cherries with white wine and crème fraiche is all that you need to expand your German menu. Simple and easy to make, this recipe is a must to try.

## Ingredients (4 servings)

1 ½ lbs. ripe black cherries un-pitted
⅔ cup fruity white wine
1 cinnamon stick
⅔ cup water
2 tablespoon sugar
Zest and juice of 1 lemon
1 ¼ cups crème fraîche
2 tablespoon Asbach Uralt

## Preparation

Crush half of the black cherries in a mortar using a pestle. Add the lemon juice, lemon peel, sugar, water, cinnamon, wine, stems, whole cherry pits, and crushed pits to a saucepan. Cover and cook for 10 minutes. Strain this liquid and return it to the pan. Stir in 1 cup crème fraiche, and half of the cherries. Next, cook for 5 minutes with occasional stirring. Puree this soup with a hand blender until smooth. Garnish the soup with the remaining cherries and crème fraiche. Enjoy.

# Seven Herb Soup

**Preparation time:** 10 minutes
**Cook time:** 10 minutes
**Nutrition facts (per serving):** 368 cal (21g fat, 8g protein, 1g fiber)

Serve the warming bowl of seven herb soup and make your meal a little more nutritional. It has everything healthy in it, ranging from cream to herbs, etc.

## Ingredients (4 servings)
1 tablespoon butter
1 small onion, chopped
1 tablespoon flour
2 cups vegetable broth
1 cup cream
2 cups fresh mixed herbs, chopped
Salt and black pepper, to taste
Croutons or cubed zwieback
Edible flowers such as dandelions or violets to garnish

## Preparation
Sauté the onions with butter in a pan until soft. Stir in flour and cook for 1 minute. Pour in the broth, mix, and cook for 3 minutes on a simmer until the soup thickens. Add the cream, chopped herbs, black pepper, and salt. Puree this soup with a hand blender then garnish with flowers. Serve warm.

# German Goulash Soup

**Preparation time:** 5 minutes
**Cook time:** 1 hour 20 minutes
**Nutrition facts (per serving):** 345 cal (21g fat, 26g protein, 2g fiber)

This rich German goulash soup is a typical German entree, which is a must to have on a healthy menu. It has this rich mix of beef with carrot and celery.

## Ingredients (8 servings)
2 tablespoon canola oil
½ lb. beef stew cubes
1 fresh onion, minced
3 cloves garlic, minced
3 tablespoon paprika
2 tablespoon tomato paste
1 cup German dry red wine
8 cups beef stock
1 large fresh carrot, sliced
1 fresh celery rib, diced
2 potatoes, peeled and chopped
Sea salt and black pepper to taste

## Preparation
Sauté the beef, onion and garlic with oil in a suitable cooking pot over medium heat until brown. Stir in the tomato paste, paprika, red wine, and beef stock. Cook the mixture to a simmer. Stir in the potatoes, celery, and carrot. Cook for 1 hour on a simmer until the vegetables and meat are soft. Adjust the seasoning with black pepper and salt. Serve warm.

# Cabbage Soup Ahrensburg

**Preparation time:** 10 minutes
**Cook time:** 25 minutes
**Nutrition facts (per serving):** 117 cal (1g fat, 5g protein, 2g fiber)

The cabbage soup is made from a mixture of white cabbage, carrots and bell peppers. You can serve this soup with your favorite crusted bread.

## Ingredients (6 servings)
3 ½ oz. bacon
3 ½ oz. onion, chopped
½ oz. cooking oil
8 ½ oz. white cabbage, shredded
7 oz. carrots, chopped
5 oz. red bell peppers, chopped
3 ½ oz. celery, chopped
1 ½ oz. spring onions, chopped
3 ⅛ cups beef broth
13 ½ oz. Hela Curry Sauce Hot

## Preparation
Sauté the bacon with the vegetables in a cooking pot for 5 minutes. Stir in the broth and cook for 20 minutes on a simmer. Add curry sauce, mix well, and serve warm.

# Beet Soup with Horseradish Yogurt

**Preparation time:** 10 minutes
**Cook time:** 30 minutes
**Nutrition facts (per serving):** 330 cal (29g fat, 7g protein, 3g fiber)

Try this German beet soup with your favorite herbs on top. Adding a dollop of cream or yogurt will make it even richer in taste.

### Ingredients (4 servings)
2 onions, chopped
⅔ oz. butter
2 oz. white wine
2 cups vegetable stock
1 ⅔ cups beets, diced
Salt, to taste
Black pepper, to taste

### *Creme fraiche*
4 ½ oz. yogurt
2 teaspoon horseradish
Watercress

### Preparation
Sauté the onion with margarine in a cooking pot until golden brown. Stir in the vegetable stock and white wine to deglaze the pot. Add the beet cubes, caraway seeds, black pepper, and salt, and then cook until the beets are soft. Puree this soup until smooth. Stir in the crème fraiche. Mix the yogurt with the horseradish in a bowl and add on top of the soup. Garnish with watercress. Serve.

# Wild Garlic Soup

**Preparation time:** 10 minutes
**Cook time:** 10 minutes
**Nutrition facts (per serving):** 125 cal (4g fat, 14g protein, 3g fiber)

Enjoy this wild garlic soup with crispy bread and a fresh vegetable salad on the side. The warming bowl of this soup makes a great serving for all the special dinners.

## Ingredients (4 servings)
3 ½ oz. wild garlic, chopped
1 cup heavy cream
Salt, to taste
1 onion, chopped
2 tablespoon butter
2 tablespoon flour
1-pint vegetable stock
1 cup milk
Black pepper, to taste
Nutmeg, to taste

## Preparation
Mix 1 tablespoon cream with a pinch of salt. Sauté the onion with butter in a soup pot until soft. Stir in the flour and sauté for 30 seconds. Pour in the vegetable stock and the milk and then mix until smooth. Stir in the wild garlic, nutmeg, sugar, black pepper, and salt. Mix well and stir in the remaining cream. Serve warm.

# Bavarian Liver Dumpling Soup

**Preparation time:** 15 minutes
**Cook time:** 30 minutes
**Nutrition facts (per serving):** 241 cal (15g fat, 22g protein, 4g fiber)

You cannot expect to have German cuisine and not try the traditional liver dumpling soup in it. This soup is full of spices and beef.

## Ingredients (6 servings)
6 oz. beef liver, chopped
7 oz. ground pork
½ loaf dried bread sliced
1 teaspoon lard
Milk, to soak the bread
½ onion chopped
1 egg
Breadcrumbs
Salt, to taste
Black pepper, to taste
Butter, to taste
Parsley, to taste
1 egg yolk
34 oz. beef broth

## Preparation
Soak the bread in milk and then cut into cubes. Mix the bread with liver, pork ground, onions, lard, butter, black pepper, salt, and egg in a bowl. Stir in the breadcrumbs and make 6 meatballs out of this mixture. Cover and refrigerate the meatballs for 1 hour. Boil the beef broth in a pan and add meatballs. Cook for 30 minutes on a simmer. Beat the egg yolk with 34oz. broth in a bowl and pour into the soup while stirring slowly. Serve warm.

# Main Dishes

# Jaeger Schnitzel

**Preparation time:** 15 minutes
**Cook time:** 40 minutes
**Nutrition facts (per serving):** 455 cal (9g fat, 39g protein, 2g fiber)

Loaded with lots of calories, Jaeger schnitzel is a German beef entrée that makes an amazing serving for all your meals. Enjoy it warm with your favorite bread.

## Ingredients (6 servings)
2 lbs. boneless pork chops, cubed
Oil for frying
2 eggs, beaten
Plain bread crumbs, to coat
3 (1 oz.) packages dry mushroom gravy mix
1-lb. fresh mushrooms, chopped
1 (16 oz.) package dry egg noodles

## Preparation
Dip the pork in beaten egg and then coat with breadcrumbs. Set a pan with cooking oil over medium heat. Sear the pork in the oil for 5-10 minutes until golden brown, then transfer to a plate. Prepare the mushroom gravy as per the package's instructions. Stir in the mushrooms and cook for 5 minutes. Boil the egg noodles in salted water until soft. Drain and add to the gravy. Mix and serve with pork chops on top. Enjoy.

# German Sautéed Spaetzle Dumplings

**Preparation time:** 10 minutes
**Cook time:** 18 minutes
**Nutrition facts (per serving):** 141 cal (6g fat, 4.7g protein, 1.2g fiber)

Try this super tasty German sautéed spaetzle recipe prepared with flour, milk, butter, etc. Serve it to your family and you'll never stop having it; that's how heavenly the combination tastes.

## Ingredients (4 servings)
1 cup all-purpose flour
¼ cup milk
2 eggs
½ teaspoon ground nutmeg
1 pinch ground white pepper
½ teaspoon salt
1-gallon hot water
2 tablespoon butter
2 tablespoon fresh parsley, chopped

## Preparation
Mix the flour, nutmeg, white pepper, and salt in a bowl. Beat the eggs with milk and pour into the flour mixture. Stir until it makes a smooth dough. Pass this dough through a spaetzle maker or a large hole sieve. Drop the spaetzle into a pot filled with simmering liquid. Cook for 8 minutes and then drain. Sauté the cooked spaetzle with butter in a cooking skillet until golden. Stir in the parsley. Serve.

# German Hamburgers (Frikadellen)

**Preparation time:** 10 minutes
**Cook time:** 30 minutes
**Nutrition facts (per serving):** 272 cal (16g fat, 22g protein, 1g fiber)

If you haven't tried the German hamburgers before, then here comes a simple and easy cook recipe that you can recreate at home in no time with minimum effort.

## Ingredients (2 servings)
1 Kaiser roll
⅔ lb. ground beef
⅓ lb. ground pork
1 onion, chopped
¼ cup fresh parsley, chopped
1 egg
1 teaspoon Hungarian hot paprika
Salt and black pepper to taste

## Preparation
Soak the Kaiser roll in a bowl filled with water for 10 minutes and then drain. Crumble this roll in a large bowl. Stir in the pork, beef, parsley, onion, egg, black pepper, salt, and paprika. Make 4 flattened hamburgers out of this mixture. Set a suitable non-stick skillet and sear the burgers for 5 minutes per side.

# German Pork Chops and Sauerkraut

**Preparation time:** 15 minutes
**Cook time:** 50 minutes
**Nutrition facts (per serving):** 363 cal (10g fat, 29g protein, 0g fiber)

This German pork chops meal is a healthy entrée that can be served with some tasty sauerkraut or coleslaw on the side, which will enhance its flavor and will make it more nutritious.

## Ingredients (8 servings)
8 center cut pork chops
2 lbs. sauerkraut, drained
1 large red apple, diced
1 onion, chopped
1 cup brown sugar
1 tablespoon caraway seeds

## Preparation
At 350 degrees F, preheat your oven. Sear the pork chops in a pan, greased with oil for 5 minutes per side. Transfer the chops to a baking dish (9x13 inch). Mix the apple, sauerkraut, brown sugar, onion, and caraway seeds in a bowl. Spread this mixture over the pork chops. Cover this dish with aluminum foil. Bake the chops for 45 minutes in the preheated oven. Serve warm.

# German Beef Rouladen

**Preparation time:** 15 minutes
**Cook time:** 40 minutes
**Nutrition facts (per serving):** 351 cal (16g fat, 45g protein, 18g fiber)

Have you tried the German beef Rouladen before? Well, here's a German delight that adds rolled beef steaks to your dinner table in a delicious way.

## Ingredients (8 servings)
¼ cup Dijon mustard
8 (4 oz.) round steaks, ¼ inch thick
½ cup onion, minced
2 teaspoon paprika
2 teaspoon salt
2 teaspoon black pepper
8 bacon slices
3 tablespoon canola oil
1 (12 oz.) can beef broth
1 ¼ cups water
2 tablespoon cornstarch
1 cup warm water
¼ cup sour cream

## Preparation
Rub ½ tablespoon mustard over the meat. Now top it with onion, salt, paprika, and a bacon slice. Roll the steaks and secure them with a toothpick. Set a pan with some canola oil over medium heat. Sear the meat roll in the pan and cook until brown from all the sides. Pour in the water and beef broth. Reduce the heat to low, cover and cook for 30 minutes. Transfer the meat rolls to the serving plate. Mix cornstarch with 1 cup water and pour into the meat broth. Stir and cook for 3 minutes until thickens. Add the sour cream and mix well. Pour this sauce on top of the rolls. Serve warm.

# Oktoberfest Chicken and Red Cabbage

**Preparation time:** 10 minutes
**Cook time:** 60 minutes
**Nutrition facts (per serving):** 271 cal (9g fat, 23g protein, 6g fiber)

Here's a simple German chicken and red cabbage recipe made with some basic ingredients. Serve this with some warm bread or rice.

## Ingredients (4 servings)

4 bacon slices
1 tablespoon bacon drippings
¼ cup all-purpose flour
½ teaspoon salt
½ teaspoon smoked paprika
2 lbs. skinless chicken thighs
1 red onion, sliced
1 large apple, cored and sliced
1 head red cabbage, cored and sliced
½ cup red wine vinegar
¼ cup dry red wine
¼ cup brown sugar
½ teaspoon ground cinnamon

## Preparation

At 350 degrees F, preheat your oven. Sear the bacon in a large skillet over medium-high heat until crispy and brown. Transfer the bacon to a plate and crumble once cooled. Mix the flour, paprika, and salt in a bowl. Coat the chicken thighs with this flour mixture and sear in the bacon fat in the same skillet for 5 minutes per side. Transfer this chicken to a plate. Add onion and apple to the same skillet. Sauté for 5 minutes, add bacon, cabbage, and a pinch of salt, and then cook for 8 minutes. Add the red wine, red wine vinegar, cinnamon, and brown sugar. Cook this mixture to a boil, reduce the heat and continue cooking for 10 minutes until reduced to half. Place the chicken thighs in this skillet. Bake the chicken for 40 minutes in the oven. Serve warm.

# Sauerbraten

**Preparation time:** 10 minutes
**Cook time:** 4 hours 20 minutes
**Nutrition facts (per serving):** 456 cal (33g fat, 41g protein, 2g fiber)

This German sauerbraten is known as the classic German dinner. The beef rump roast with thick gravy tastes heavenly with rice and bread.

## Ingredients (6 servings)
3 lbs. beef rump roast
2 large onions, chopped
1 cup red wine vinegar
1 cup water
1 tablespoon salt
1 tablespoon black pepper
1 tablespoon white sugar
10 whole cloves
2 bay leaves
2 tablespoon all-purpose flour
Salt and black pepper to taste
2 tablespoon vegetable oil
10 gingersnap cookies, crumbled

## Preparation
Add the beef rump roast, bay leaves, cloves, sugar, 1 tablespoon black pepper, 1 tablespoon salt, water, vinegar, and onions to a large cooking pot. Cover and refrigerate this mixture for 3 days. Remove the meat from the marinade and pat it dry. Mix the flour with black pepper and salt. Coat the beef with the flour mixture and shake off the excess. Set a Dutch oven over medium heat and stir in vegetable oil. Sear the beef in the hot oil for 10 minutes until brown. Pour the marinade over the beef and reduce the heat to medium low. Cook for 4 hours until meat is soft. Remove the meat from sauce and slice. Strain the remaining

broth and return it to the cooking pot. Stir in the gingersnap cookies and cook for 10 minutes until the sauce thickens. Return the beef to the sauce. Mix and serve warm.

# Wienerschnitzel

**Preparation time:** 10 minutes
**Cook time:** 12 minutes
**Nutrition facts (per serving):** 515 cal (27g fat, 29g protein, 1.2g fiber)

Wienerschnitzel offers another popular entrée known for its crispy veal cutlets. Serve with toasted burgers and salad.

## Ingredients (4 servings)
1½ lb. veal cutlets
½ cup all-purpose flour
3 tablespoon Parmesan cheese, grated
2 eggs
1 teaspoon parsley, minced
½ teaspoon salt
¼ teaspoon black pepper
1 pinch ground nutmeg
2 tablespoon milk
1 cup dry bread crumbs
6 tablespoon butter
4 lemon slices

## Preparation
Wrap the veal cutlet in between two plastic sheets and pound them with a mallet into ¼ inch thickness. Coat the cutlet with flour and shake off the excess. Mix Parmesan cheese with milk, nutmeg, black pepper, salt, parsley, and eggs se in a medium bowl. Spread the breadcrumbs on a plate. Coat the cutlet with egg mixture and then coat with the breadcrumb's mixture. Cover and refrigerate the veal for 1 hour. Set a large skillet over medium heat and add butter to melt. Sear the cutlet in the butter for 3 minutes per side. Garnish with lemon slices and pan juices. Enjoy.

# Pork Roast with Sauerkraut and Potatoes

**Preparation time:** 15 minutes
**Cook time:** 10 hours
**Nutrition facts (per serving):** 386 cal (15g fat, 31g protein, 1g fiber)

If you haven't tried the famous pork roast with sauerkraut and potatoes before, then here comes a simple and easy cook recipe that you can recreate at home in no time with minimum effort.

## Ingredients (6 servings)
6 white potatoes, peeled and quartered
1 tablespoon garlic, minced
Salt and black pepper to taste
1 (3 lbs.) boneless pork loin roast
1 (32 oz.) jar sauerkraut with liquid
2 teaspoon caraway seeds

## Preparation
Add the potatoes, black pepper, salt, and garlic to a slow cooker. Top with the sauerkraut and caraway seeds. Cover and cook on low heat for 10 hours. Serve warm.

# Pork Shanks (Grillhaxe)

**Preparation time:** 10 minutes
**Cook time:** 3 hours
**Nutrition facts (per serving):** 532 cal (28g fat, 270 protein, 1g fiber)

Make these pork shanks at home in no time and enjoy it with some garnish on top. Adding a drizzle of paprika on top makes it super tasty.

## Ingredients (6 servings)
1 cup olive oil
2 tablespoon dried marjoram
2 tablespoon dried basil
2 tablespoon fresh thyme, chopped
2 tablespoon fresh rosemary, chopped
2 tablespoon sea salt
1 teaspoon paprika
1 teaspoon black pepper
1 teaspoon vegetable bouillon powder
6 (1 ½ lb.) pork shanks

## Preparation
At 350 degrees F, preheat your oven. Mix olive oil with bouillon powder, black pepper, paprika, salt, thyme, rosemary, basil, marjoram, and olive oil in a bowl. Add the pork shanks to this mixture and mix well to coat. Place the shanks on a baking sheet and roast for 3 hours in the oven. Serve warm.

# German Chicken

**Preparation time:** 15 minutes
**Cook time:** 30 minutes
**Nutrition facts (per serving):** 236 cal (17g fat, 29 protein, 2g fiber)

This quick and easy Germs chicken recipe is also quite famous in the region; in fact, it's a must to try because of its nutritional content.

## Ingredients (4 servings)
4 boneless chicken breast halves
1 cup barbecue sauce
22 oz. sauerkraut

## Preparation
At 350 degrees F, preheat your oven. In a 9x13 inch baking dish, place the sauerkraut in a single layer. Place the prepared chicken breasts on top of the sauerkraut. Pour the barbecue sauce over the chicken. Cover and bake the chicken in the preheated oven for 30 minutes or until the chicken is cooked and the juices run clear.

# North German Kale and Sausage

**Preparation time:** 10 minutes
**Cook time:** 53 minutes
**Nutrition facts (per serving):** 388 cal (11g fat, 28g protein, 3g fiber)

This German kale and sausage are everything you must be looking for to make you dinner loaded with nutrients. The combination of crispy bacon, ham, and kale make a complete package.

## Ingredients (4 servings)

1 lb. kale, stemmed and chopped
3 bacon slices, diced
½ onion, chopped
2 cups water, or as needed to cover
2 teaspoon beef bouillon granules
¼ teaspoon ground nutmeg
1 tablespoon prepared mustard
½ lb. thickly sliced cooked ham
4 links kielbasa sausage
Salt and black pepper to taste

## Preparation

Boil the kale in a pot filled with boiling water for 1 minute and then drain. Sauté the bacon in a large skillet for 8 minutes over medium heat. Stir in the onion and then sauté for 5 minutes. Add the kale and cook for 4 minutes. Pour in enough water to cover and cook to a boil. Reduce the heat, add beef bouillon granules, and nutmeg. Cook for 30 minutes. Next, add mustard, ham slices, and sausage links on top. Cook for 35 minutes and then adjust seasoning with black pepper and salt. Serve warm.

# German Kielbasa

**Preparation time:** 15 minutes
**Cook time:** 15 minutes
**Nutrition facts (per serving):** 519 cal (12g fat, 20g protein, 2g fiber)

This German kielbasa loved by all, young and adult. It's simple and quick to make. This delight is great to serve at dinner tables.

## Ingredients (6 servings)

6 apples, peeled, cored and chopped
1 (32 oz.) package sauerkraut
¼ cup brown sugar
2 lbs. kielbasa sausage, sliced

## Preparation

Mix the apples and sauerkraut in a large skillet over medium heat and cook for 10 minutes. Stir in the sugar and the kielbasa. Finally, cook for 5 minutes. Serve warm.

# Schweinshaxe

**Preparation time:** 10 minutes
**Cook time:** 3 hours 30 minutes
**Nutrition facts (per serving):** 566 cal (43g fat, 26g protein, 0.8g fiber)

Here come the famous Schweinshaxe which is a pork knuckles recipe. The knuckles are first cooked in a brine solution and then baked for a crispy texture.

## Ingredients (2 servings)
1 carrot, diced
1 onion, peeled and diced
1 leek, chopped
1 stalk celery, diced
2 meaty pork knuckles
2 tablespoon vegetable shortening
1 teaspoon whole black peppercorns
Salt, to taste
¼ cup beer
1 pinch ground cumin

## Preparation
Add the pork knuckles, celery, leek, onion, and carrot to a large stockpot. Stir in the salt, peppercorns, and enough water to cover the pork. Cover and cook for 3 hours on medium heat, then remove the knuckles from the heat. At 425 degrees F, preheat your oven. Add shortening to a cooking pan and melt it. Stir in the pork knuckles, cooked veggies, and 2 cups of the cooking liquid. Bake these pork knuckles for 30 minutes in the oven. Add beer and cumin. Mix well and serve warm.

# German Lasagna

**Preparation time:** 10 minutes
**Cook time:** 50 minutes
**Nutrition facts (per serving):** 303 cal (18g fat, 14g protein, 0.4g fiber)

If you want something exotic and delicious on your dinner menu, then nothing can taste better than this German kielbasa lasagna.

## Ingredients (6 servings)
9 lasagna noodles
1 (10 ⅔ oz.) can cream of mushroom soup
1 (10 ⅔ oz.) can cream of chicken soup
2 cups of milk
1-lb. kielbasa
1 (20 oz.) can sauerkraut, drained
8 oz. mozzarella cheese, shredded

## Preparation
At 375 degrees F, preheat your oven. Boil pasta in a pot filled with salted water for 10 minutes then drain. Blend the mushroom soup with milk and cream of chicken soup in a blender. Add 1 cup soup mixture in a 9x13 inches baking pan. Place 3 lasagna strips on top in a single layer. Add half of the sauerkraut, half of the sausage, and ⅓ cheese on top. Repeat the layers and finally top them with 3 pasta strips and the remaining soup mixture. Cover these layers with a foil sheet and bake for 25 minutes in the oven. Uncover and bake for 15 minutes. Garnish with the remaining cheese and serve.

# Slow Cooker Apple Pork Chops

**Preparation time:** 15 minutes
**Cook time:** 5 hours 10 minutes
**Nutrition facts (per serving):** 337 cal (18g fat, 28g protein, 2g fiber)

If you haven't tried the famous apple pork chops before, then here comes a simple and easy to cook recipe that you can recreate at home in no time with minimum efforts.

## Ingredients (6 servings)
1 tablespoon canola oil
6 bone-in pork chops
½ cup apple juice
¼ cup apple cider vinegar
1½ cups chicken broth
1 tablespoon brown sugar
½ teaspoon meat tenderizer
½ teaspoon garlic powder
¼ teaspoon ground nutmeg
¼ teaspoon ground ginger
¼ teaspoon black pepper
2 Granny Smith apples, cored and sliced
1 sweet onion, sliced
¼ head cabbage, shredded

## Preparation
Sear the pork chops in a skillet with canola oil for 5 minutes per side. Mix black pepper, ginger, nutmeg, garlic powder, meat tenderizer, brown sugar, chicken broth, cider vinegar, and apple juice in a slow cooker. Place the pork chops in the cooker, and top them with cabbage, onion, and apple. Cover and cook on low heat for 5 hours with occasional stirring. Serve warm.

# Pork Roast with Apples

**Preparation time:** 15 minutes
**Cook time:** 4 hours
**Nutrition facts (per serving):** 338 cal (9g fat, 28g protein, 0g fiber)

Basically a spicy baked pork roast recipe with an apple, it's renowned for its super-nutritious blend of ingredients. It tastes great when served with a dollop of cream or yogurt.

## Ingredients (6 servings)

1 (3 lbs.) pork loin roast
1 (20 oz.) can sauerkraut, drained
2 large apples, cored and quartered
2 large onions, quartered
⅓ cup brown sugar
1 (12 oz.) can beer

## Preparation

At 250 degrees F, preheat your oven. Place the pork roast in a large baking dish and top it with sauerkraut. Add apple and onion quarters around the roast. Add the remaining ingredients on top. Cover this dish with a foil sheet and bake for 4 hours in the preheated oven. Serve warm.

# German Spaghettini

**Preparation time:** 5 minutes
**Cook time:** 85 minutes
**Nutrition facts (per serving):** 424cal (21g fat, 21g protein, 1g fiber)

The German Spaghettini is loved by all due to its amazing blend of spaghettini, sausage, and tomatoes. This meal makes an irresistible serving for the table.

## Ingredients (4 servings)
1-lb. lean ground beef
¼ lb. Italian sausage
6 bacon slices
1 (15 oz.) can tomato sauce
1 (28 oz.) can canned tomatoes
⅓ cup white sugar
12 oz. spaghettini

## Preparation
Sauté the beef in a skillet until brown and then transfer to a plate. Sauté the sausage in the same skillet until brown. Stir in the browned beef, bacon, tomato sauce, sugar, and tomatoes and then cook for 45 minutes on a simmer. Boil the pasta in a pan filled with boiling salted water for 10 minutes, then drain. At 300 degrees F, preheat your oven. Add the cooked spaghettini to the meat mixture. Spread the pasta in a casserole dish and bake for 30 minutes in the oven. Serve warm.

# Butter Dumplings

**Preparation time:** 15 minutes
**Cook time:** 10 minutes
**Nutrition facts (per serving):** 261 cal (22g fat, 14 protein, 2g fiber)

This German butter dumplings recipe is a must to have on this German menu. It has an easy mix of butter, eggs, and flour.

## Ingredients (4 servings)

14 tablespoon butter
4 eggs
1 ¾ cups flour
½ teaspoon salt
¼ teaspoon nutmeg

## Preparation

Beat the butter in a bowl until fluffy. Stir in the eggs and mix well. Add the dry ingredients and mix well. Cover and refrigerate for 30 minutes. Boil water for cooking the dumplings in a pot. Take 2 teaspoon of the prepared dough at a time and shape it into a triangle dumpling. Make more dumplings and add them to the water. Cook the dumplings for 5 minutes, drain, and serve.

# Baked Fish

**Preparation time:** 15 minutes
**Cook time:** 35 minutes
**Nutrition facts (per serving):** 493 cal (15g fat, 30g protein, 1.7g fiber)

A perfect mix of sole fillet with apple, horseradish, and sour cream is a must to try. Serve warm with your favorite side salad for the best taste.

## Ingredients (2 servings)
1 ½ lb. sole filet
2 tablespoon vinegar
1 tablespoon butter, melted
4 tablespoon horseradish, grated
1 apple, grated
¾ cup sour cream
Salt, to taste

## Preparation
At 350 degrees F, preheat your oven. Grease a casserole dish with butter. Place the fish in this dish and drizzle vinegar and melted butter on top. Bake the fish fillets for 5 minutes. Mix the rest of the ingredients in a bowl and pour over the fish. Lastly, bake for 30 minutes. Serve warm.

# Smoked Salmon and Leek Strudel

**Preparation time:** 10 minutes
**Cook time:** 40 minutes
**Nutrition facts (per serving):** 428 cal (18g fat, 26g protein, 1g fiber)

Have you tried the smoked salmon and leek strudel before? Well, now you can enjoy this unique and flavorsome combination by cooking this recipe at home.

## Ingredients (2 servings)
4 tablespoon olive oil
6 shallots, sliced
4 leeks, cut into ½ inch slices
½ cup dry cider
3 ½ oz. light cream cheese
Juice ½ lemon
3 ½ oz. Smoked salmon, chopped
4 filo pastry sheets
Plain flour to dust
Chopped parsley to garnish

## Preparation
At 350 degrees F, preheat your oven. Sauté 1 tablespoon oil with leeks and shallots in a cooking skillet for 10 minutes on low heat. Stir in the cider and cook until reduced to half. Add the salmon, black pepper, and salt. Brush the filo sheet with cooking oil and place them on over another. Add the salmon filling at the center of the pastry and fold the layers over the filling to make a strudel. Place this strudel in a baking sheet, greased with cooking oil and bake for 30 minutes until golden brown. Drizzle parsley on top. Garnish with lemon wedges and green veggies. Serve warm.

# Chilli And Pepper Meatloaf

**Preparation time:** 15 minutes
**Cook time:** 55 minutes
**Nutrition facts (per serving):** 352 cal (24g fat, 31g protein, 0.6g fiber)

This meatloaf is so delicious and perfect to complete your menu, especially on a nutritious diet. It's best to make a large number of servings.

## Ingredients (8 servings)
1 pita bread
1 tablespoon vegetable olive oil
1 onion, chopped
2 green chillies, chopped
3 garlic cloves, chopped
1 teaspoon ground cumin
1 teaspoon ground coriander
½ teaspoon ground cinnamon
1 tablespoon smoked paprika
8 ½ oz. jar roasted red peppers, drained
21 oz. beef minced
9 oz. lamb mince
Grated zest and juice of 1 lemon
2 tablespoon tomato purée
Handful fresh parsley, chopped
1 large egg

## Preparation
At 350 degrees F, preheat your oven. Grind the pita bread in a food processor until crumbly. Sauté the onion with oil in a frying pan until soft. Stir in the garlic and chilies and then sauté for 1 minute. Add the spices, cook for 1 minute, and then remove from the heat. Chop ⅔ peppers and mix with the onion mixture, egg, parsley, tomato puree, lemon zest, and lemon juice, lamb, beef and pita

crumbs in a bowl. Spread the beef mixture in a greased loaf pan. Place this pan in a roasting pan and pour some boiling water into the tin. Bake the meatloaf for 45 minutes in the oven. Garnish with the remaining peppers, lemon zest, and parsley. Serve warm.

# Salmon, Cream Cheese and Watercress Rolls

**Preparation time:** 15 minutes
**Nutrition facts (per serving):** 357 cal (9g fat, 24g protein, 3g fiber)

Now you can quickly make flavorsome salmon and cream cheese rolls at home and serve it to have a fancy meal for yourself and your guest.

## Ingredients (6 servings)
4 tablespoon light cream cheese
2 tablespoon soured cream
1 tablespoon lemon juice
1 teaspoon fresh dill, chopped
16 smoked salmon strips
Bunch of fresh chives, snipped
1 oz. watercress stems discarded

## Preparation
Mix cream cheese, sour cream, and lemon juice in a bowl. Stir in dill and mix well. Place half of the salmon strips on a working surface. Divide half of the cheese mixture on top of the salmon. Add half of the watercress on top. Roll the salmon strip and repeat the same steps with the remaining strips. Place these rolls in a box and cover to refrigerate for 1 hour. Garnish with lemon wedges and watercress. Serve.

# Kohlrabi with Soured Cream and Dill

**Preparation time:** 10 minutes
**Cook time:** 35 minutes
**Nutrition facts (per serving):** 416 cal (28g fat, 17g protein, 1g fiber)

Let's make some kohlrabi with soured cream and dill with these simple ingredients. Mix them together and then cook to create a great combination of flavors.

## Ingredients (6 servings)
1 tablespoon butter
1 tablespoon vegetable oil
4 kohlrabies, peeled and sliced
3 large carrots, cut into chunks
¼ teaspoon smoked paprika
1 cup fresh vegetable stock, hot
⅔ cup carton soured cream
1 small bunch of fresh dill, chopped

## Preparation
Sauté the kohlrabi with butter, oil, carrots, paprika and salt in a cooking pan for 5 minutes. Stir in the stock, reduce the heat, cover, and cook for 30 minutes with occasional stirring. Stir in the soured cream and add the dill. Mix well and serve warm.

# Potato and Sauerkraut Gratin

**Preparation time:** 10 minutes
**Cook time:** 70 minutes
**Nutrition facts (per serving):** 326 cal (17g fat, 23g protein, 2g fiber)

This potato and sauerkraut gratin entrée will melt your heart away with its epic flavors. The streaky bacon with juniper berries, potatoes, and sauerkraut o make it taste even better and nutritious.

## Ingredients (6 servings)
1 tablespoon butter, lard or duck fat
7 ½ oz. smoked streaky bacon, diced
2 onions, sliced
1 teaspoon juniper berries, crushed
1 teaspoon green peppercorns, crushed
1 bay leaf
3 tablespoon sauerkraut
6 medium waxy potatoes, sliced
½ cup white wine or cider
¾ cup light vegetable stock
3 tablespoon crème fraiche

## Preparation
Sauté the bacon with butter in a cooking pan until crispy and brown. Stir in the spices, bay leaf, and onions. Cover and cook for 8 minutes with occasional stirring. Fold in the sauerkraut and mix well. Cook the potatoes slices in salted water for 5 minutes and then drain. At 350 degrees F, preheat your oven. Add wine to the onion mixture and cook for 3 minutes. Stir in the stock and cook for 8 minutes with occasional stirring. Remove from the heat and then add the crème fraiche. Spread the potatoes and onion mixture in a casserole in layer and cover with the foil. Bake these layers for 50 minutes in the oven. Serve warm.

# Cheat's Beef Stroganoff

**Preparation time:** 10 minutes
**Cook time:** 14 minutes
**Nutrition facts (per serving):** 379 cal (18g fat, 31g protein, 6g fiber)

This beef stroganoff recipe has unique flavors due to its rich blend of rice, steak, and mushrooms. Serve warm with your favorite bread on the side.

## Ingredients (4 servings)
8 oz. long grain rice
18 oz. beef steaks, cut into strips
1 teaspoon mixed peppercorns, crushed
1 tablespoon olive oil
1 onion, sliced
5 oz. mushrooms wiped and halved
¾ cup carton sour cream
2 teaspoon paprika

## Preparation
Cook the long-grain rice as per the package's instructions, then drain. Place the beef strips in a bowl and add the crushed peppercorns on top. Sauté the onion slices with olive oil in a cooking skillet for 4 minutes. Stir in the mushrooms and cook for 5 minutes. Toss in the beef strips and sauté for 5 minutes until brown. Stir in 3 tablespoon water and cook until it bubbles. Add the sour cream, paprika, and mix well. Serve warm with rice.

# Frankfurter Roll with New Potato and Bierwurst Salad

**Preparation time:** 15 minutes
**Cook time:** 15 minutes
**Nutrition facts (per serving):** 393 cal (3g fat, 14g protein, 7g fiber)

If you haven't tried the frankfurter roll with new potato and bierwurst salad, then here comes a simple and easy to cook recipe that you can recreate at home in no time with minimum efforts.

**Ingredients (6 servings)**
4 jumbo frankfurters or hot dogs
4 bread rolls
1 oz. butter softened
A handful of rocket leaves
German mustard, to taste
Ketchup, to taste

*Salad*
18 oz. waxy new potatoes, halved
5 oz.bierwurst sausage, sliced thickly
3 spring onions, sliced diagonally
1 dessert apple, cut into chunks
2 gherkins, sliced
4 radishes, sliced
Chopped fresh chives, to garnish

**Dressing**
1 tablespoon quark (yogurt cheese)
3 tablespoon mayonnaise
1 tablespoon German mustard
2 tablespoon olive oil
1 teaspoon sugar

**Preparation**

Boil the potatoes in a pot filled with salted boiling water for 15 minutes and then remove them. Add the frankfurters (or hot dogs) to the water, cook until hot, and then drain. Meanwhile, mix all the dressing ingredients in a bowl and then toss in all the salad ingredients. Cut the rolls in half and divide the frankfurters, rocket leaves, ketchup, and mustard into the rolls and serve with salad.

# German Classic Meatloaf

**Preparation time:** 15 minutes
**Cook time:** 65 minutes
**Nutrition facts (per serving):** 319cal (14g fat, 28g protein, 7g fiber)

German meatloaf with bacon, beef and pork is one option to go for. Plus, if you have the pork and beef ready in your refrigerator, you can make it in no time.

## Ingredients (8 servings)
2 tablespoons milk
1 large egg
1 oz. soft white bread
1 small red onion, chopped
1 garlic clove, crushed
1 celery stick, chopped
1 oz. butter
3 ½ oz. rindless bacon, chopped
14 oz. beef minced
14 oz. pork mince
1 tablespoon German mustard
2 large gherkins, chopped
1 teaspoon fresh thyme, chopped
2 tablespoon fresh parsley, chopped
Grated fresh nutmeg

## Preparation
At 350 degrees F, preheat your oven. Mix the egg with milk in a large bowl. Add the bread, soak for 15 minutes, and then mash it. Sauté the onion, celery, and garlic with butter in a suitable skillet on low heat until soft, then transfer to a plate. Add the bacon to the same skillet and sauté until crispy. Add the onion mixture, gherkins, mustard, pork, beef and crispy bacon to the bread, along with

spices and herbs. Mix well and spread this meat mixture into a loaf pan. Bake the meatloaf for 50 minutes in the oven. Slice and serve warm.

# Kaiserschmarrns

**Preparation time:** 15 minutes
**Cook time:** 6 minutes
**Nutrition facts (per serving):** 277 cal (24g fat, 10g protein, 3g fiber)

If you want some new and exotic flavors in your meals, then this Kaiserschmarrns recipe is best to bring that variety to the menu.

## Ingredients (6 servings)
1 ½ cup flour
4 eggs
1 pinch salt
1 cup milk
2 teaspoon lemon juice
½ cup cranberries
Powdered sugar, to serve
Oil for cooking

## Preparation
Beat the egg whites separately in a bowl until fluffy. Mix flour with the egg yolks and milk until smooth. Stir in the salt, lemon juice, and egg white. Mix gently and then fold in the cranberries. Add 1-2 tablespoon oil to a cooking pan over medium heat. Pour enough batter to get ½ inch thick layer in the pan and cook until set. Flip and cook for 2-3 minutes. Scramble the pancake and transfer it to a plate. Repeat the same steps with the remaining batter. Garnish with sugar and enjoy.

# Chicken, Sausage and Sauerkraut

**Preparation time:** 10 minutes
**Cook time:** 52 minutes
**Nutrition facts (per serving):** 492 cal (39g fat, 32g protein, 1.2g fiber)

Here's another classic German recipe for your dinner and lunch. Serve it with delicious bread and enjoy the best of it.

### Ingredients (6 servings)
1 tablespoon olive oil
4 bone-in chicken thighs
½ teaspoon salt
½ teaspoon black pepper
14 oz. kielbasa sausage, cut into slices
1 medium onion, sliced
1 ¼ lb. medium Yukon gold potatoes, cut into slices
2 cups sauerkraut, drained, rinsed
1 cup chicken broth
Sour cream, to taste

### Preparation
Rub the chicken with ¼ teaspoon black pepper, and ¼ teaspoon salt. Place this chicken in the Dutch oven with the cooking oil. Sear the chicken for 11 minutes until golden brown from both sides. Transfer it to a plate. Add the kielbasa to the Dutch oven and sauté for 3 minutes, then transfer to a plate. Add the onion and sauté for 8 minutes. Add the sauerkraut, potatoes, kielbasa, broth, remaining salt, and black pepper. Return the chicken on top, cover, and cook for 30 minutes on a simmer. Serve warm.

# Pork Cutlets with Apple Slaw

**Preparation time:** 15 minutes
**Cook time:** 20 minutes
**Nutrition facts (per serving):** 392 cal (18g fat, 29g protein, 1g fiber)

Are you in a mood to have pork cutlets on the menu? Well, you can try these pork cutlets with apple slaw for a change and see how tasty they are.

## Ingredients (4 servings)
### Pork Cutlets
4 boneless pork loin chops, ½ inch thick
8 saltine crackers, crushed
½ cup Bisquick mix
½ teaspoon paprika
¼ teaspoon black pepper
1 egg
1 tablespoon water
Cooking spray

### Apple Slaw
4 cups coleslaw mix
1 small tart red apple, chopped
¼ cup onion, chopped
⅓ cup coleslaw dressing
⅛ teaspoon celery seed

## Preparation
Mix all the ingredients for apple slaw in a bowl, cover, and refrigerate until the pork chops are ready. At 425 degrees F, preheat your oven. Grease 15x10 inch pan with cooking spray. Layer it with wax paper. Pound the pork chop with a mallet into ¼ inch thickness. Mix the crackers, black pepper, paprika, and Bisquick mix in a bowl. Beat the egg with water in a bowl. Dip the pork chops

in the egg mixture and coat with the Bisquick mixture, and repeat the coating layers. Place the pork chops on a baking sheet and then bake for 20 minutes in the oven. Serve warm with apple slaw.

# Chicken with Creamy Paprika Sauce

**Preparation time:** 10 minutes
**Cook time:** 38 minutes
**Nutrition facts (per serving):** 344 cal (41g fat, 34g protein, 3g fiber)

This chicken with creamy paprika sauce will leave you drooling and craving for more. Try serving it with warm tortillas.

## Ingredients (5 servings)
10 chicken thighs
1 medium onion, sliced
3 tablespoon chicken broth
2 tablespoon paprika
½ teaspoon salt
3 cups uncooked egg noodles
3 tablespoon cornstarch
3 tablespoon cold water
1 container (8 oz) sour cream

## Preparation
Add the chicken, onion, broth, paprika, and salt to a slow cooker. Next, cover and cook on low heat for 8 hours. Cook the noodles in the last 20 minutes as per the package's instructions. Transfer the chicken to a plate. Mix the cornstarch with water and pour into the gravy. Cook for 10 minutes on high heat until it thickens. Add the potato topper, mix well, and pour over the chicken. Serve warm with noodles.

# German-Style Pasta

**Preparation time:** 15 minutes
**Cook time:** 7 minutes
**Nutrition facts (per serving):** 309 cal (12g fat, 17g protein, 3g fiber)

Do you want to enjoy some pasta with a German twist? Then try this recipe and enjoy the best of all flavors in one single meal.

## Ingredients (4 servings)

1 cup uncooked rotini pasta
2 teaspoon vegetable oil
4 cups red cabbage, shredded
1 tablespoon packed brown sugar
2 tablespoon white vinegar
½ teaspoon Caraway seed
¼ teaspoon salt
Ground black pepper, to taste

## Preparation

Cook the pasta as per the package's instruction and then drain. Sauté the cabbage with oil in a cooking pot for 2 minutes. Stir in the brown sugar, caraway seed, and vinegar then cover and cook for 5 minutes. Add the pasta and adjust the seasoning with black pepper and salt. Serve warm.

# Baked Cheesy Spaetzle Pasta

**Preparation time:** 15 minutes
**Cook time:** 40 minutes
**Nutrition facts (per serving):** 400 cal (11g fat, 5g protein, 4g fiber)

The saucy and baked spaetzle pasta German will melt your heart with its great taste and texture. Serve warm with white rice.

## Ingredients (4 servings)
9 oz. German Spaetzle pasta
1 large onion, sliced
1 ½ cups Emmenthal cheese
4 tablespoon butter
Salt and black pepper to taste

## Preparation
At 400 degrees F, preheat your oven. Cook the pasta as per the package's instruction and keep it aside. Sauté the onion with butter in a pan until soft. Stir in black pepper and salt and then cook until caramelized. Remove this mixture from the heat. Spread the pasta in a 9x9 inch baking dish, top it with cooked onions and ¾ cheese, and then repeat the layers. Bake for 30 minutes in the oven. Serve warm.

# Klump

**Preparation time:** 10 minutes
**Cook time:** 47 minutes
**Nutrition facts (per serving):** 286 cal (13g fat, 19g protein, 2g fiber)

Let's have a rich and delicious combination of potatoes, pearls, and mashed potatoes. Bake it home and serve warm with white sauce and cheese on top.

## Ingredients (8 servings)
2 lbs. floury potatoes
3 ½ oz. butter
5 oz. bacon lardons
1 large onion
2 ripe pears, cored and chopped
14 oz. kale
Handful cheddar, grated

## Preparation
Boil the potatoes in salted water in a cooking pot until soft then drain. Sauté the butter with bacon in a skillet until golden. Stir in the onion and sauté until soft. Blanch the kale leaves in a pot filled with boiling water for 2 minutes then drain. Chop the leaves and add to the bacon mixture. Add 2 tablespoon water, black pepper, cover and cook for 15 minutes on low heat. At 350 degrees F, preheat your oven. Peel the cooked potatoes and mash them with the remaining butter and seasoning in a bowl. Spread the kale mixture in a gratin dish and top this layer with potato mash. Drizzle cheese on top and bake for 20 minutes in the oven. Serve warm.

# German Bread Dumplings

**Preparation time:** 15 minutes
**Cook time:** 20 minutes
**Nutrition facts (per serving):** 225 cal (4g fat, 14g protein, 1g fiber)

This German bread dumpling is one of the German specialties, and everyone must try this interesting combination of soaked bread rolls, onion, and milk.

## Ingredients (8 servings)
14 rolls, cubed
1 onion, chopped
1 bunch parsley, chopped
3 tablespoon butter
2 cups milk
6 eggs
1 ½ tablespoon salt
½ teaspoon black pepper
¼ cup bread crumbs

## Preparation
Sauté the onions with butter in a cooking pan until soft. Stir in the parsley and sauté for 1 minute. Remove from the heat and pour in the milk. Mix well and pour this mixture over the bread cubes. Beat the egg with black pepper and salt in a bowl. Pour this over the bread and leave for 15 minutes. Mix well and knead for 2 minutes. Stir in the breadcrumbs and make small balls from this mixture. Boil water in a cooking pan and cook the dumplings in this water for 20 minutes. Finally, transfer to a plate. Serve warm.

# German Green Beans (Speckbohnen)

**Preparation time:** 15 minutes
**Cook time:** 20 minutes
**Nutrition facts (per serving):** 265 cal (13g fat, 13g protein, 0.2g fiber)

You can't really imagine a German menu with having a green beans meal in it. Now you can prepare it using some sautéed green beans and bacon.

## Ingredients (2 servings)
6 oz. green beans
½ tablespoon butter
¼ onion
⅔ oz. bacon

## Preparation
Add the green beans to a large bowl and pour boiling water over them. Leave for 2 minutes and then drain. Sauté the onion with butter in a cooking pot until soft. Stir in the bacon and sauté until crispy. Add the green beans, cook for 1 minute, and then serve warm.

# Desserts

# German Apfelkuchen

**Preparation time:** 15 minutes
**Cook time:** 55 minutes
**Nutrition facts (per serving):** 295 cal (11g fat, 6g protein, 1g fiber)

The delicious Apfelkuchen will satisfy your sweet cravings in no time. They're quick to make if you have cake batter ready at home.

## Ingredients (6 servings)
### Cake
1 ½ cups all-purpose flour
¾ cup sugar
2 teaspoon baking powder
½ teaspoon salt
⅛ teaspoon nutmeg
¼ cup cold butter
½ cup milk
1 egg
4 apples, sliced
¼ cup almonds, sliced
¼ cup dried currants

### Custard
1 cup heavy cream
2 teaspoon flour
½ cup sugar
1 egg
1 teaspoon vanilla extract
1 teaspoon cinnamon
1 pinch salt

## Preparation

At 400 degrees F, preheat your oven. Mix the flour with salt, baking powder, and sugar in a mixing bowl. Add in the butter and mix until crumbly. Beat the milk with the egg and then pour into the flour mixture. Mix well until lump-free. Pour the batter into a 9-inch springform pan. Top this batter with apple slices and bake for 20 minutes in the preheated oven. Meanwhile, for custard, mix ¼ cream with flour in a bowl until smooth. Stir in the salt, cinnamon, vanilla, egg, sugar, and the remaining cream. Pour this custard batter on top of the cake and sprinkle currants and almond on top. Bake again for 35 minutes at 350 degrees F. Allow the cake to cool and then slice to serve.

# German Bee Sting Cake (Bienenstich Kuchen)

**Preparation time:** 15 minutes
**Cook time:** 35 minutes
**Nutrition facts (per serving):** 360 cal (14g fat, 8g protein, 1g fiber)

This bee sting cake makes an easy way to enjoy a fancy dessert, and this recipe will let you bake a delicious cake in no time.

### Ingredients (8 servings)
*Cake*
1 ¾ cup flour
2 tablespoon sugar
2 teaspoon yeast
1 pinch of salt
1 egg
¼ cup butter, melted
⅓ cup milk

*Topping*
½ cup butter
1 tablespoon honey
6 tablespoon sugar
1 ½ tablespoon heavy whipping cream
1 tablespoon vanilla sugar
¾ cup almonds, sliced

*Filling*
2 cups heavy whipping cream
3 tablespoon vanilla pudding powder
1 teaspoon vanilla sugar

## Preparation

Mix the flour, salt, yeast, and sugar in a mixing bowl. Beat the egg with milk and melted butter in a bowl and pour into the flour mixture. Mix well to form a smooth dough. Knead this dough for 7 minutes, transfer to a bowl, and cover with a plastic sheet. Leave the prepared dough for 30 minutes. At 350 degrees F, preheat your oven. For the almond topping, mix the melted butter with vanilla sugar, sugar, and honey in a saucepan over medium-low heat and cook for 1 minute. Stir in the cream and mix well. Remove the topping from the heat and add sliced almonds. Layer an 8x8 inch baking pan with parchment paper. Spread the prepared dough in the pan and top this crust with the almond topping. Bake it for 30-35 minutes until golden brown. Allow the cake to cool. Mix cream with vanilla sugar and pudding powder in a bowl until fluffy. Slice the cake in half and spread the cream mixture on top of the bottom layer. Place the other cake layer on top. Slice and serve.

# German Raspberry Dessert

**Preparation time:** 10 minutes
**Cook time:** 10 minutes
**Nutrition facts (per serving):** 319 cal (10g fat, 5g protein, 4g fiber)

Count on this German raspberry dessert to make your dessert menu extra special and surprise your loved one with the ultimate flavors.

## Ingredients (4 servings)
10 oz. raspberries, frozen
3 pumpernickel bread slices
2 oz. dark chocolate, chopped
2 tablespoon Chambord raspberry liquor
2 tablespoon cherry juice
½ cup whipping cream
10 oz. yogurt
2 tablespoon sugar
1 tablespoon vanilla

## Preparation
Blend the pumpernickel in a food processor until crumbly. Add the chopped chocolate and pour schnapps to soak this mixture. Beat the cream in a bowl until creamy. Stir in the yogurt, vanilla, and sugar. Divide the soaked bread mixture into the serving cups and top this layer with the cream mixture. Garnish with raspberries. Cover and refrigerate for 1 hour. Serve.

# Spaghetti Ice Cream

**Preparation time:** 5 minutes
**Nutrition facts (per serving):** 353 cal (18g fat, 7g protein, 4g fiber)

Simple and easy to make, this spaghetti ice cream is a must to try on this menu. German ice cream dessert is a delight to add to your dessert menu when covered with berry sauce.

## Ingredients (6 servings)
1 tub vanilla ice cream
8 oz. strawberries, quartered
1 tablespoon of sugar
2 teaspoon orange juice
White chocolate shavings
Whipped cream

## Preparation
Blend the strawberries with sugar in a blender. Stir in the orange juice and blend for 5 minutes. Cover and refrigerate this mixture until cool. Grate the white chocolate and keep it aside. Pass the ice cream through a potato ricer into the serving cups. Top the noodles with strawberry sauce and white chocolate. Serve.

# Christmas Stollen With Almonds

**Preparation time:** 15 minutes
**Cook time:** 50 minutes
**Nutrition facts (per serving):** 292 cal (9g fat, 11g protein, 4g fiber)

The German Christmas stollen with almond isn't only delicious, but it also makes a healthy and loaded dessert. You can serve this stollen dessert with hot beverages.

## Ingredients (6 servings)

3 ½ oz. mixed dried fruit with peel
¾ cup apple juice
¼ oz. dried yeast
9 oz. plain flour
1 tablespoon blanched whole almonds
1 pinch of ground cinnamon
1 pinch of ground aniseed
1 small pinch ground cloves
3 ½ oz. cold marzipan, cut into small pieces
2 teaspoon butter, melted
1 tablespoon icing sugar

## Preparation

Soak all the dried fruit in ½ cup hot water and then drain. Heat the apple juice in a pan and then remove from the heat. Stir in the yeast and leave for 15 minutes. Add flour, and mix well until smooth. Cover this dough and leave for 2 hours. Add dried fruit, spices, nuts, and marzipan to the prepared dough and mix knead it well. Shape dough into a log and place it in a baking sheet lined with baking parchment paper. Cover it with a kitchen towel. Leave the prepared dough for 1 hour. At 360 degrees F, preheat your oven. Bake the stolen for 20 minutes in the oven. Reduce the heat to 300 degrees F and bake for 25 minutes until golden brown. Dust it with icing sugar, slice, and serve.

# German Rum Balls (Rumkugeln)

**Preparation time:** 15 minutes
**Cook time:** 10 minutes
**Nutrition facts (per serving):** 255 cal (6g fat, 11g protein, 3g fiber)

Here's a delicious and savory combination of hazelnuts, chocolate, and sugar in the rum balls. All the right ingredients are mixed in a perfect balance to give you a great dessert.

## Ingredients (6 servings)
7 tablespoon unsalted butter
¾ cup powdered sugar sieved
2 tablespoon rum
7oz. chocolate, chopped
7oz. peeled and toasted hazelnuts, ground
2 tablespoon cocoa powder

## Preparations
Add chocolate to a bowl and melt by heating in the microwave. Toast the hazelnuts in a pan until golden and then grind in a food processor. Beat butter in a bowl until fluffy. Stir in powder sugar and beat again. Stir in the rum and mix well. Add the melted chocolate and mix until smooth. Add the ground hazelnuts, mix well, cover, and refrigerate for 30 minutes. Make small balls from this mixture and roll the balls in cocoa powder and powdered sugar. Serve.

# German Peach Kuchen

**Preparation time:** 15 minutes
**Cook time:** 45 minutes
**Nutrition facts (per serving):** 297 cal (16g fat, 11g protein, 4g fiber)

If you haven't tried the German peach kuchen before, then here comes a simple and easy to cook recipe that you can recreate at home in no time with minimum efforts.

## Ingredients (6 servings)
### Crust
½ cup unsalted cold butter
2 cups all-purpose flour
¼ teaspoon baking powder
½ teaspoon salt

### Filling
1 cup granulated sugar
12 peach halves
1 teaspoon cinnamon
2 egg yolks
1 cup heavy cream

## Preparation
At 400 degrees F, preheat your oven. Mix butter, baking powder, flour, 2 tablespoon sugar, and salt in a bowl until crumbly. Spread this mixture in an 8-inch baking pan. Spread peach halves on top. Mix the remaining sugar with cinnamon in a bowl and drizzle over the peaches. Bake the kuchen for 15 minutes in the oven. Beat the egg yolks with cream in a bowl and pour over the peaches. Bake again for 30 minutes. Allow the kuchen to cool and serve.

# German Plum Dumplings (Zwetschgenknoedel)

**Preparation time:** 15 minutes
**Cook time:** 25 minutes
**Nutrition facts (per serving):** 370 cal (17g fat, 5g protein, 3g fiber)

Enjoy delicious, juicy, sweet, and savory plum dumplings with the help of this recipe. Serve with honey or lemon glaze on top.

## Ingredients (8 servings)
1 cup quark (yogurt cheese)
10 tablespoon butter
3 tablespoon sugar
1 teaspoon lemon zest
1 egg
¾ cup flour
¼ teaspoon baking powder
1 dash salt
12 plums, pitted and cut in half
12 sugar cubes
5 pieces of Zwieback, crushed
½ cup cinnamon sugar

## Preparation
Drain the quark to remove excess liquid. Mix the quark with 3 tablespoon of sugar and 7 tablespoons of butter in a bowl until smooth. Stir in the lemon zest and the egg. Stir in the salt, baking powder, and flour. Next, mix well until smooth. Wrap this dough with a plastic sheet and refrigerate for 1 hour. Boil salted water in a cooking pot. Add an ice cube at the center of plum halves in place of the plum's pit. Wrap each plum with 1/12th portion of the prepared dough. Add the plum dumplings to the hot water and cook for 25 minutes. Remove the dumplings from the water and transfer them to a plate. Mix the

remaining butter with bread crumbs and sugar. Coat the dumplings with a breadcrumb mixture. Drizzle cinnamon and sugar on top. Serve.

# German Blueberry Cheesecake (Heidelbeerkuchen)

**Preparation time:** 15 minutes
**Cook time:** 60 minutes
**Nutrition facts (per serving):** 345 cal (22g fat, 15g protein, 1g fiber)

The famous blueberry cheesecake is here to make your German cuisine extra special. Serve them with some maple syrup on top.

## Ingredients (8 servings)
### Berries
6 ½ cups fresh blueberries
Batter
4 oz. Neufchatel cheese
1 tablespoon milk
1 egg
4 tablespoon vegetable oil
¼ cup granulated sugar
4 teaspoon Vanilla sugar
1 pinch salt
1 ⅔ cup flour
4 teaspoon baking powder

### Topping
2 tablespoon butter
½ cup of sugar
8 oz. Neufchatel cheese
1 egg
4 teaspoons Vanilla sugar
1 tablespoon cornstarch
5 tablespoons cold milk

## Preparation

At 350-degree F, preheat your oven. Grease a 9-inch springform pan. Blend the cheese with milk, egg, sugar, oil, salt, and vanilla sugar in a mixer until smooth. Stir in the baking powder, flour, and then mix well until smooth. Spread this dough in the baking pan, up to 2 inches from its walls. Spread blueberries in the crust. Add milk and cornstarch to the cheese mixture and mix until smooth. Pour this mixture over the berries and bake for 60 minutes in the oven. Allow the cheesecake to cool. Slice and serve.

# German Cheesecake (Käsekuchen)

**Preparation time:** 10 minutes
**Cook time:** 60 minutes
**Nutrition facts (per serving):** 391 cal (51g fat, 13g protein, 2g fiber)

Have you ever tried the German cheesecake? If not, then here comes a recipe that will help you cook the finest cheesecake in no time.

**Ingredients (8 servings)**
*Crust*
1 ½ cups flour
1 teaspoon baking powder
1 pinch of salt
2 teaspoon vanilla sugar
1 tablespoon lemon rind, grated
¼ cup granulated sugar
6 tablespoon butter
1 egg, beaten

*Filling*
3 egg yolks
¾ cup granulated sugar
2 teaspoon vanilla sugar
6 tablespoon butter
¾ cup heavy cream
2 cups quark (Greek yogurt)
1 ½ teaspoon cornstarch
3 egg whites
1 pinch of salt

## Preparation

Mix the flour, vanilla, sugar, lemon zest, salt, and baking powder in a bowl. Add in the butter and mix until crumbly. Stir the egg and mix well to make dough. Wrap the prepared dough with a plastic sheet and refrigerate for 1 hour. Roll the prepared dough into a 9-inch round and spread in a 9inch springform pan. Prepare the filling and beat the egg yolks with vanilla sugar, sugar, and butter in a bowl until smooth. Stir in the cream and mix well. Stir in the quark and mix well. Beat the egg whites with salt in a bowl until fluffy. Add the egg whites to the batter along with cornstarch. Mix evenly and spread the batter on top of the crust. Bake the cheesecake for 60 minutes at 300 degrees F. Allow the cake to cool and serve.

# German Coconut Macaroons (Kokosmakronen)

**Preparation time:** 10 minutes
**Cook time:** 15 minutes
**Nutrition facts (per serving):** 230 cal (23g fat, 12g protein, 1g fiber)

Crispy and creamy, soft and fluffy, these German macaroons are so full of surprise. IN essence, you'll cherish the sweet taste.

## Ingredients (8 servings)
4 oz. coconut flakes
9 oz. sugar
4 egg whites
1 oz. flour
Baking wafers (1 ½ inch in diameter)
½ lemon, zest
Chocolate frosting (for decoration)

## Preparation
Prepare a hot water bath. Beat the egg whites with sugar in a bowl. Place this bowl over hot water and mix until the sugar is dissolved. Stir in the coconut flakes and mix well. Cook this mixture at 325 degrees F with frequent stirring. Remove the mixture from the heat and stir in flour. Mix well, then add lemon peel. At 320 degrees F, preheat your oven. Spread the baking wafers on a baking sheet. Divide the prepared dough over the wafers into macarons and bake for 10 minutes. Leave in the oven for 5 minutes after baking. Serve with chocolate frosting on top.

# German Fruit Flan

**Preparation time:** 15 minutes
**Cook time:** 20 minutes
**Nutrition facts (per serving):** 396 cal (23g fat, 8g protein, 0g fiber)

If you haven't tried the delicious German flan before, then here comes a simple and easy cook this recipe that you can recreate at home in no time with minimum efforts.

## Ingredients (6 servings)

6 tablespoon all-purpose flour
6 tablespoon granulated sugar
6 tablespoon neutral oil
1½ teaspoon baking powder
3 large eggs

## Preparation

At 360 degrees F, preheat your oven. Grease an 11-inch flan pan. Mix flour with sugar, oil, baking powder, and eggs in a bowl and beat for 5 minutes with a hand mixer. Spread the batter in the pan and bake for 15 minutes in the oven until golden brown. Allow the flan to cool and serve.

# Sweet Venison Cake

**Preparation time:** 10 minutes
**Cook time:** 35 minutes
**Nutrition facts (per serving):** 248 cal (13g fat, 9g protein, 6g fiber)

This sweet venison cake makes an excellent dessert serving! It's loved by all, young and adult, due to its delicious mix of biscuits, almonds, and sugar.

## Ingredients (6 servings)
9 oz. Zwieback biscuits
9 tablespoon butter
5 oz. of sugar
4 eggs
3 ½ oz. ground almonds
2 tablespoon flour
1 teaspoon baking powder

## *Garnish*
3 ½ oz. dark chocolate
2 tablespoon coconut oil
2 oz. almonds for garnish

## Preparation
At 350 degrees F, preheat your oven. Grate the biscuits in a food processor and add the ground almonds, baking powder, and flour. Next, mix well. Beat butter, sugar, and eggs in a bowl. Pour this mixture into the flour mixture. Mix well and spread this mixture in a greased baking pan. Bake the cake for 35 minutes at 350 degrees F in the preheated oven. Allow the cake to cool; meanwhile, prepared the glaze with melted chocolate with coconut oil in a bowl by heating in the microwave. Pour this glaze over the cake and garnish it with almonds. Slice and serve.

# Strawberry Rhubarb Trifle

**Preparation time:** 15 minutes
**Cook time:** 10 minutes
**Nutrition facts (per serving):** 384 cal (19g fat, 5g protein, 1.4g fiber)

Try this rhubarb trifle dessert, and enjoy the best of the savory flavors. The recipe is simple and gives you lots of nutrients in one place.

## Ingredients (6 servings)
1 lb. rhubarb, peeled and chopped
⅝ cup sugar
1 cup heavy cream
1 lb. strawberries
2 ½ oz. meringues
Lemon balm leaves for garnish

## Preparation
Cook the rhubarb with ⅓ cup sugar in a saucepan and cook for 10 minutes with occasional stirring. Allow this mixture to cool. Puree the rhubarb with a masher. Stir in whipped cream and mix evenly. Mix ¾ strawberries with the remaining sugar in a bowl. Break the large meringues into pieces and divide them into serving glasses. Top the pieces with the strawberry mixture and rhubarb cream. Garnish with any remaining strawberry. Serve.

# Drinks

# Dark Hot Chocolate
# (Zartbitter Heisse Schokolade)

**Preparation time:** 5 minutes
**Cook time:** 5 minutes
**Nutrition facts (per serving):** 279 cal (11g fat, 9g protein, 6g fiber)

This dark hot chocolate is known as a classic German holiday drink. The chocolaty drink is a warming delight.

### Ingredients (1 serving)
1 cup of whole milk
1 tablespoon of dark cocoa powder
1 tablespoon of vanilla sugar
½ oz. of bittersweet, chopped
A pinch of salt
½ teaspoon of cornstarch

### Preparation
Mix the chocolate with sugar, salt, milk ,and dark cocoa in a saucepan and cook on medium with continuous stirring until it boils. Serve.

# Apple Cider (Apfelschorle)

**Preparation time:** 5 minutes
**Nutrition facts (per serving):** 150 cal (0g fat, 0g protein, 2g fiber)

The German apple cider drink, also known as Apfelschorle, is famous for its amazing blend of ice, apple cider, and carbonated water.

## Ingredients (1 serving)
½ glass apple juice, cold
½ glass carbonated water, cold

## Preparation
Fill half of the beer glass with sprite or lemon soda. Pour in beer and add ice cubes. Serve.

# German Glühwein

**Preparation time:** 10 minutes
**Cook time:** 21 minutes
**Nutrition facts (per serving):** 172 cal (0g fat, 1g protein, 0g fiber)

The German glühwein drink is famous for its blend of orange, sugar, and red wine. You can prep this drink easily at home with this basic recipe.

### Ingredients (4 servings)
½ medium orange
¾ cup of water
¼ cup turbinado sugar
20 whole cloves
2 cinnamon sticks
2 whole star anise
1 (3 cup) bottle dry red wine
Rum or amaretto, for serving

### Preparation
Mix all the ingredients to a saucepan and cook for 1 minute on a simmer. Reduce the heat and cook for 20 minutes on a simmer. Strain and serve.

# White German Drink

**Preparation time:** 5 minutes
**Nutrition facts (per serving):** 131 cal (0g fat, 1g protein, 1.4g fiber)

Have this white German drink and enjoy the best of the Kahlua flavors in this drink. Serve it chilled for best taste.

## Ingredients (2 servings)
1 oz. vodka
1 oz. Kahlua
5 oz. milk
1 splash Jägermeister (herbal liqueur)

## Preparation
Fill a highball glass with ice. Pour vodka and Kahlua on top. Pour in Jägermeister and milk. Serve.

# German Punch (Kinderpunsch)

**Preparation time:** 5 minutes
**Cook time:** 15 minutes
**Nutrition facts (per serving):** 120 cal (0g fat, 1g protein, 1g fiber)

Here's a special German Christmas punch made with orange juice, apple juice, and cherry juice, so it's super refreshing.

## Ingredients (6 servings)
2 cups orange juice
2 cups apple juice
½ cup cherry juice
2 cups of water
2 cinnamon sticks
10 whole cloves
2 whole star anise
5 bags of hibiscus tea
Honey to taste

## Preparation
Mix all the liquids and whole spices in a saucepan. Cook the mixture to a boil, reduce the heat, and cover to cook for 15 minutes. Add the tea bags to the drink, remove them from the heat, and cover them. Leave the tea for 15 minutes. Strain and serve.

# Feuerzangenbowle

**Preparation time:** 5 minutes
**Cook time:** 5 minutes
**Nutrition facts (per serving):** 136 cal (0g fat, 2g protein, 1.3g fiber)

Made from red wine and orange juice, this beverage is a refreshing addition to the German cocktail menu.

## Ingredients (8 servings)

8 cups red wine
2 cups orange juice
1 orange, sliced
1 lemon, untreated
1 stick cinnamon
6 cloves
4-star anises
1 sugar cone
1 ½ cups rum, more than 50%

## Preparation

Heat the wine in a saucepan and stir in orange and lemon juice and spices. Cook the drink for 5 minutes on low heat and then strain. Garnish with orange slices. Serve.

# German Christmas Punch (Weihnachtspunsch)

**Preparation time:** 5 minutes
**Cook time:** 20 minutes
**Nutrition facts (per serving):** 122 cal (0g fat, 1g protein, 0 g fiber)

This refreshing sweet Christmas punch is always a delight to serve at parties. Now you can make it easily at home by using the following simple ingredients.

## Ingredients (6 servings)
5 tablespoon brown sugar
Juice from one lemon
1 (3 cups) bottle red wine
2 cups orange juice
2 cups black tea
1 ½ teaspoon vanilla extract
1 lemon sliced
1 orange sliced
1 cinnamon stick
8 whole cloves
7 tablespoon marzipan
1 oz. semi-sweet chocolate
¾ cup rum

## Preparation
Mix all the punch ingredients in a saucepan and cook for 20 minutes with occasional stirring. Remove cinnamon stick, cloves, lemon slices, and orange slices from the drink. Serve.

# German Vacation Drink

**Preparation time:** 5 minutes
**Nutrition facts (per serving):** 161 cal (0g fat, 3g protein, 1g fiber)

This German vacation drink is a great beverage to serve at any time. It offers a unique blend of Jägermeister and gold rum.

**Ingredients (4 servings)**
1 oz. Jägermeister
1 oz. Old gold rum
¾ oz. Domaine de Canton ginger liqueur
¾ oz. Orgeat
¾ oz. lemon juice
3 dashes Peychaud's bitters
Lime wedge
Candied ginger

**Preparation**
Shake all the liquid ingredients in a cocktail shaker and pour into a glass filled with ice. Garnish with a lime wedge and candied ginger. Serve.

If you liked German recipes, discover to how cook DELICIOUS recipes from **Balkan** countries!

Within these pages, you'll learn 35 authentic recipes from a Balkan cook. These aren't ordinary recipes you'd find on the Internet, but recipes that were closely guarded by our Balkan mothers and passed down from generation to generation.

Main Dishes, Appetizers, and Desserts included!

If you want to learn how to make Croatian green peas stew, and 32 other authentic Balkan recipes, then start with our book!

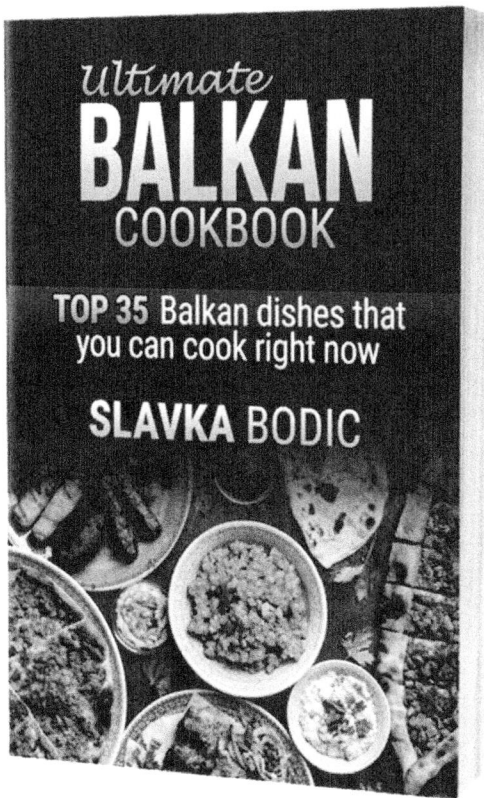

Order at www.balkanfood.org/cook-books/ for only $2,99

If you're a **Mediterranean** dieter who wants to know the secrets of the Mediterranean diet, dieting, and cooking, then you're about to discover how to master cooking meals on a Mediterranean diet right now!

In fact, if you want to know how to make Mediterranean food, then this new e-book - "The 30-minute Mediterranean diet" - gives you the answers to many important questions and challenges every Mediterranean dieter faces, including:

- How can I succeed with a Mediterranean diet?
- What kind of recipes can I make?
- What are the key principles to this type of diet?
- What are the suggested weekly menus for this diet?
- Are there any cheat items I can make?

... and more!

If you're serious about cooking meals on a Mediterranean diet and you really want to know how to make Mediterranean food, then you need to grab a copy of "The 30-minute Mediterranean diet" right now.

Prepare **111 recipes with several ingredients in less than 30 minutes**!

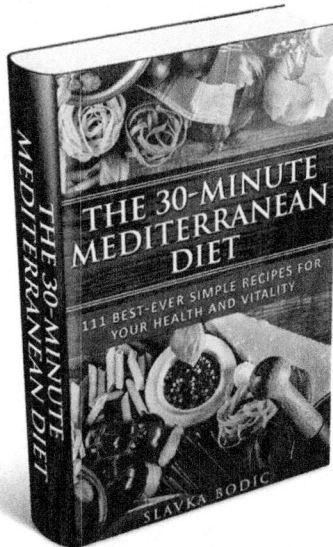

Order at www.balkanfood.org/cook-books/ for only $2,99

What could be better than a home-cooked meal? Maybe only a **Greek** homemade meal.

Do not get discouraged if you have no Greek roots or friends. Now you can make a Greek food feast in your kitchen.

This ultimate Greek cookbook offers you 111 best dishes of this cuisine! From more famous gyros to more exotic *Kota Kapama* this cookbook keeps it easy and affordable.

All the ingredients necessary are wholesome and widely accessible. The author's picks are as flavorful as they are healthy. The dishes described in this cookbook are "what Greek mothers have made for decades."

Full of well-balanced and nutritious meals, this handy cookbook includes many vegan options. Discover a plethora of benefits of Mediterranean cuisine, and you may fall in love with cooking at home.

Inspired by a real food lover, this collection of delicious recipes will taste buds utterly satisfied.

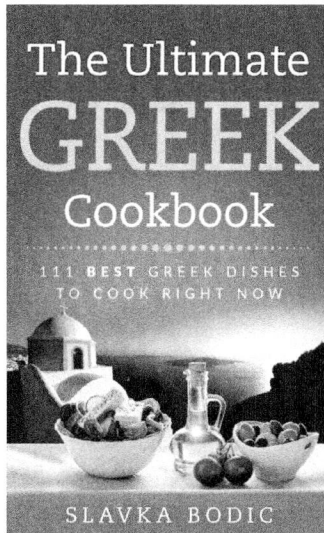

The Ultimate
GREEK
Cookbook
111 BEST GREEK DISHES
TO COOK RIGHT NOW
SLAVKA BODIC

Order at www.balkanfood.org/cook-books/ for only $2,99

Maybe to try exotic **Syrian** cuisine?

From succulent *sarma*, soups, warm and cold salads to delectable desserts, the plethora of flavors will satisfy the most jaded foodie. Have a taste of a new culture with this **traditional Syrian cookbook**.

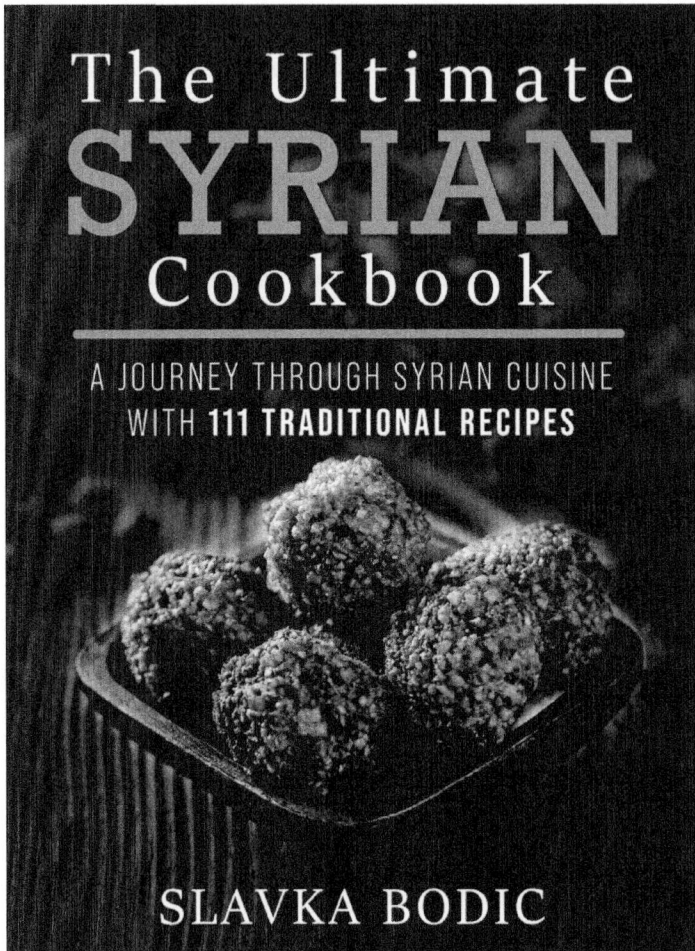

Order at www.balkanfood.org/cook-books/ for only $2,99

Maybe **Polish** cuisine?

# The Ultimate POLISH Cookbook

**MASTER 111 TRADITIONAL**
DISHES FROM POLAND

SLAVKA BODIC

Order at www.balkanfood.org/cook-books/ for only $2,99

Or **Peruvian**?

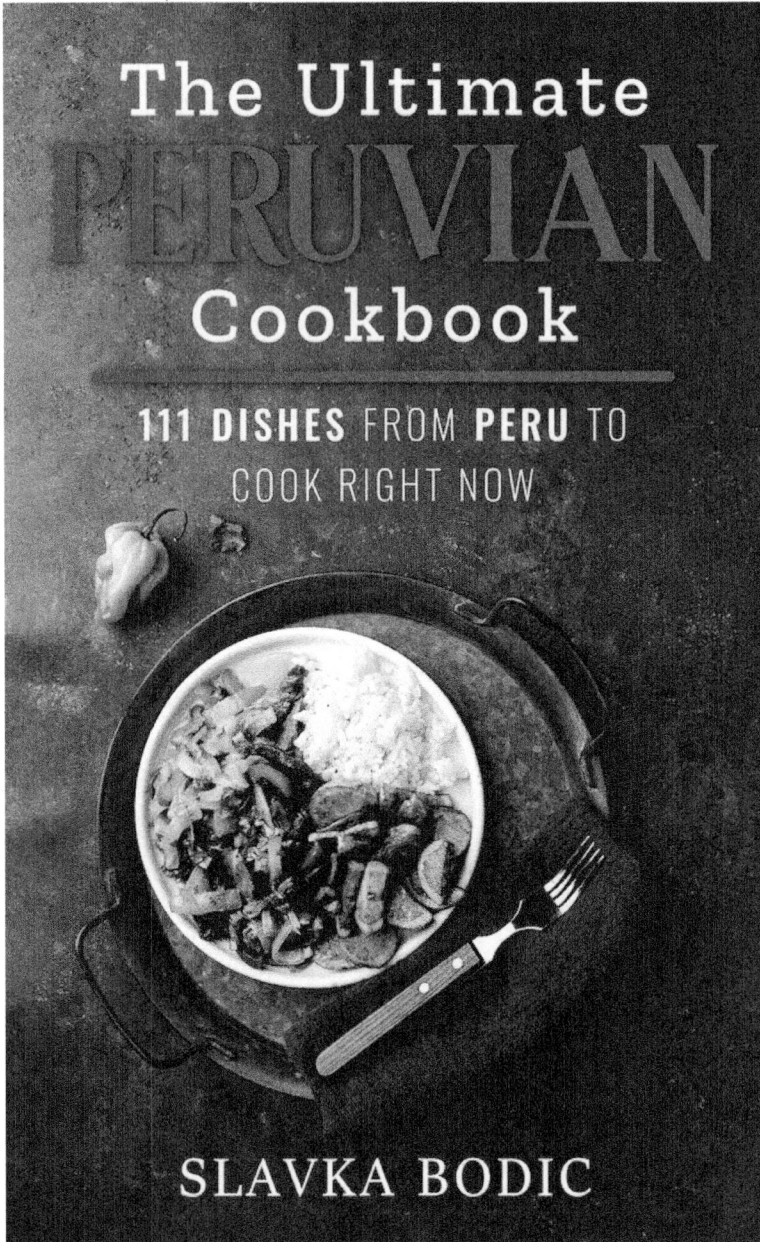

Order at www.balkanfood.org/cook-books/ for only $2,99

# ONE LAST THING

If you enjoyed this book or found it useful, I'd be very grateful if you could find the time to post a short review on Amazon. Your support really does make a difference and I read all the reviews personally, so I can get your feedback and make this book even better.

Thanks again for your support!

Please send me your feedback at

www.balkanfood.org

Printed in Great Britain
by Amazon